North Carolina Legal Research

CAROLINA ACADEMIC PRESS
LEGAL RESEARCH SERIES

Suzanne E. Rowe, Series Editor

❧

Arizona, Second Edition—Tamara S. Herrera

Arkansas—Coleen M. Barger

California, Second Edition—Hether C. Macfarlane, Aimee Dudovitz
& Suzanne E. Rowe

Colorado—Robert Michael Linz

Connecticut—Jessica G. Hynes

Federal—Mary Garvey Algero, Spencer L. Simons, Suzanne E. Rowe,
Scott Childs & Sarah E. Ricks

Florida, Fourth Edition—Barbara J. Busharis, Jennifer LaVia
& Suzanne E. Rowe

Georgia—Nancy P. Johnson, Elizabeth G. Adelman & Nancy J. Adams

Idaho—Tenielle Fordyce-Ruff & Suzanne E. Rowe

Illinois, Second Edition—Mark E. Wojcik

Iowa—John D. Edwards, M. Sara Lowe, Karen L. Wallace
& Melissa H. Weresh

Kansas—Joseph A. Custer & Christopher L. Steadham

Kentucky—William A. Hilyerd, Kurt X. Metzmeier & David J. Ensign

Louisiana, Second Edition—Mary Garvey Algero

Massachusetts—E. Joan Blum

Michigan, Second Edition—Pamela Lysaght & Cristina D. Lockwood

Minnesota—Suzanne Thorpe

Mississippi Legal Research—Kristy L. Gilliland

Missouri, Second Edition—Wanda M. Temm & Julie M. Cheslik

New York, Second Edition—Elizabeth G. Adelman, Theodora Belniak
& Suzanne E. Rowe

North Carolina, Second Edition—Scott Childs & Sara Sampson

Ohio—Katherine L. Hall & Sara Sampson

Oklahoma—Darin K. Fox, Darla W. Jackson & Courtney L. Selby

Oregon, Third Edition—Suzanne E. Rowe

Pennsylvania—Barbara J. Busharis & Bonny L. Tavares

Tennessee—Sibyl Marshall & Carol McCrehan Parker

Texas, Revised Printing—Spencer L. Simons

Washington, Second Edition—Julie Heintz-Cho, Tom Cobb
& Mary A. Hotchkiss

West Virginia—Hollee Schwartz Temple

Wisconsin—Patricia Cervenka & Leslie Behroozi

Wyoming—Debora A. Person & Tawnya K. Plumb

❧

North Carolina Legal Research

Second Edition

Scott Childs
Sara Sampson

Suzanne E. Rowe, Series Editor

CAROLINA ACADEMIC PRESS

Durham, North Carolina

Library of Congress Cataloging-in-Publication Data

Childs, Scott, author.
North Carolina legal research / Scott Childs, Sara Sampson. -- Second edition.
    p. cm. -- (Legal research series)
Includes bibliographical references and index.
ISBN 978-1-61163-616-1 (alk. paper)
1. Legal research--North Carolina. I. Sampson, Sara, author. II. Title.

KFN7475.C48 2014
340.072'0756--dc23

                         2014010575

CAROLINA ACADEMIC PRESS
700 Kent Street
Durham, North Carolina 27701
Telephone (919) 489-7486
Fax (919) 493-5668
www.cap-press.com

Printed in the United States of America.

Summary of Contents

Chapter 1 · Foundation for Legal Research and Analysis   3

Chapter 2 · The Research Process: Strategies and Techniques   11

Chapter 3 · Researching Secondary Sources   33

Chapter 4 · Researching Constitutions   55

Chapter 5 · Researching Statutes   61

Chapter 6 · Researching Legislative History   77

Chapter 7 · Researching Judicial Opinions   97

Chapter 8 · Researching Administrative Rules and Decisions   127

Chapter 9 · Updating Research   143

Chapter 10 · Researching North Carolina Court Rules and
Rules of Ethics   159

Epilogue · Revisiting the Research Process   167

Appendix A · North Carolina Routes of Appeal   171

Appendix B · Geographic Boundaries of the United States
Judicial System   173

Appendix C · Legal Citation   175

About the Authors   193

Index   195

Contents

List of Tables and Figures   xix

Series Note   xxiii

Preface and Acknowledgments   xxv

Chapter 1 · Foundation for Legal Research and Analysis   3

I. North Carolina Legal Research   3

II. The Role of Legal Analysis in Legal Research   3

III. Types of Legal Authority   4
    A. Primary Authority   4
        1. Mandatory Authority   5
        2. Persuasive Authority   5
    B. Secondary Authority   5
    C. Distinctions of Authority within Primary, Mandatory Authority   6

IV. Court Systems   7
    A. North Carolina Courts   7
    B. Federal Courts   8
    C. Courts of Other States   9

V. Organization of This Text   9

Chapter 2 · The Research Process: Strategies and Techniques   11

I. Overview of the Research Process   11

II. Planning a Research Strategy   13
    A. Getting Started   13

1. Gathering Facts and Identifying Issues   13
2. Determining Jurisdiction   13
3. Generating Research Terms   13
B. What Legal Information Do You Need?   15
C. Choosing Between Print and Online Sources of
   Legal Information   15
   1. Availability   15
   2. Cost   16
   3. Accuracy   17
   4. Age   17
   5. Context   17
   6. Efficiencies   18
   7. Confidentiality   18
D. Strategies for Research in Print Sources   18
   1. Using Known Citations or Names to Locate
      Specific Documents   19
      a. Using Citations to Specific Publications   19
      b. Using the Proper Name of a Litigant or an Act 19
   2. Browsing Tables of Contents   20
   3. Browsing an Index for a Specific Legal Term   20
   4. Browsing Pocket Parts and Supplements to Update   20
E. Strategies for Research in Online Sources   21
   1. Overview of Commercial Research Services   21
   2. Using Known Citations to Locate Specific Documents 23
   3. Browsing Online by Topic   24
      a. Browsing on WestlawNext   24
      b. Browsing on Lexis Advance   24
      c. Key Number Digest of Case Law on WestlawNext   24
      d. Tables of Contents of Specific Sources   24
   4. Keyword Searching   25
      a. Methods and Strategies for Full-text Keyword Searching 25
      b. Keyword Searching an Online Index Database   28
      c. Keyword Searching a Field or Segment of Each
         Document in a Database   28
   5. Natural Language Searching   29

III. Interconnectedness of Legal Information   29

IV. Organizing and Modifying the Research Process   30

Appendix   30

The Difference Between Search Terms for Indexes and Digests
   vs. Search Terms for Online Searching   30

Chapter 3 · Researching Secondary Sources   33

I. Introduction   33
   A. The Role of Secondary Sources in the Legal Research Process   33
   B. Secondary Sources and Practice Materials   34
   C. Selecting the Most Relevant Secondary Source   34
   D. Online vs. Print   36

II. Legal Encyclopedias   36
   A. *Strong's North Carolina Index*   36
      1. Researching with Print   36
      2. Researching with Strong's on Westlaw   38
   B. *American Jurisprudence, 2d*   38
      1. Researching with Print   38
      2. Researching with Westlaw and Lexis   38
   C. *Corpus Juris Secundum*   39
      1. Researching with Print   39
      2. Researching with Westlaw   39

III. Treatises, Practice Guides, and Other Books   39
   A. *Nutshells*   39
   B. Hornbooks   40
   C. Professional Treatises   40
   D. North Carolina Treatises   40
   E. Finding Treatises   41

IV. Legal Periodicals   41
   A. Free Access on the Internet   42
   B. Print Indexes   43
   C. Online Indexes   43
   D. Full-text Articles on Westlaw and Lexis   44
   E. HeinOnline   44
   F. Google Scholar   45
   G. Other Types of Legal Periodicals   45
   H. The Research Process for Periodicals   46

V. *American Law Reports*   46
   A. ALR Annotations   46
   B. How to Research an Issue in ALR   47

VI. Restatements and Principles — American Law Institute   48
    A. The Creation of Restatements and Principles   48
    B. Researching an Issue in the Restatements or Principles   50

VII. Continuing Legal Education Publications   50

VIII. Legal Forms   51

IX. Jury Instructions   52

X. Uniform Laws and Model Codes   53

XI. Law-related Blogs   54

Chapter 4 · Researching Constitutions   55

I. Researching the 1971 North Carolina Constitution   57

II. Interpreting the North Carolina Constitution   58

III. Researching the United States Constitution   58

IV. Interpreting the United States Constitution   59

Chapter 5 · Researching Statutes   61

I. Forms of North Carolina Statutory Law   61
    A. Session Laws   62
    B. Codes   62
        1. *General Statutes of North Carolina Annotated*   63
        2. *West's North Carolina General Statutes Annotated* 64
        3. North Carolina General Statutes from the General Assembly   64
        4. North Carolina General Statutes on Bloomberg Law   65

II. Initial Print Research Strategy   65
    A. Using a Citation or Popular Name   65
    B. Browsing the Index for Search Terms   66
    C. Browsing the Table of Contents for the Chapters   66

III. Initial Online Research Strategy   66
    A. Using a Citation or Popular Name   67
    B. Browsing the Index of the Code Online   67
    C. Searching the Code by Keyword   67
    D. Browsing Chapters as a Table of Contents   68

IV. Continued Research Strategy Regardless of Format   68

A. Read Statutory Law 68
B. Find and Read Cases Interpreting the Statute 69
C. Interpret and Apply the Statute to the Facts 70

V. Researching Statutes of Other States 70

VI. Researching Federal Statutes 71
A. *United States Code* 72
B. *United States Code Annotated* and *United States Code Service* 72
C. Print Research Strategies for Federal Statutes 73
    1. Retrieving by Citation or Popular Name 73
    2. Searching the Index 73
    3. Browsing the Titles 74
D. Online Research Strategies for Federal Statutes 74
    1. Using a Citation or Popular Name to Search the United States Code 74
    2. Browsing the Index of the United States Code Online 74
    3. Searching the Code by Keyword 75
    4. Browsing Titles as a Table of Contents 75

Chapter 6 · Researching Legislative History 77

I. Introduction to the North Carolina Legislative Process 78

II. Tracking Current North Carolina Legislation 78
A. The General Assembly Website 78
    1. Tracking by Bill Number 78
    2. Other Tracking Options on the Website 83
B. Other Online Sources for Tracking North Carolina Legislation 83
    1. WestlawNext 83
    2. Lexis Advance 83
    3. Bloomberg Law 84
C. Calling or Visiting the Bill Status Desk 84
D. Other Options for Tracking Current North Carolina Legislation 84
    1. Legislative Week in Review 84
    2. Legislative Reporting Services from the University of North Carolina School of Government 84

III. Researching North Carolina Legislative History 85
A. Why Research Legislative History? 85
B. Methods of Researching Legislative History 86
    1. State Sources 86

a. Session Law Number   86
b. Session Law Text   86
c. Final Bill and Previous Versions   87
d. Pre-1985 Bill Reports   87
e. Committee Minutes   88
f. Floor Debate   88
g. Study Reports   88
h. Governor's Statements   89
2. WestlawNext and Lexis Advance as Sources of
Legislative History   90

IV. Federal Legislation   90
A. Summary of the Federal Legislative Process   90
B. Tracking Current United States Legislation   91
1. Using Congress.gov to Track Federal Legislation   92
2. Other Online Sources for Tracking Federal Legislation   92
a. Govtrack.us   93
b. WestlawNext   93
c. Lexis Advance   93
d. Bloomberg Law   93
C. Researching Federal Legislative History   93
1. Why Research Federal Legislative History?   93
2. Shortcuts: Legislative History Available in the
Annotated Codes   94
3. Shortcuts: Compiled Histories   94
4. Shortcuts: Committee Reports   94
5. Collecting Your Own Legislative History   94

Chapter 7 · Researching Judicial Opinions   97

I. Court Systems   97
A. North Carolina Courts   97
1. Trial Courts in North Carolina   98
2. North Carolina Court of Appeals   98
3. North Carolina Supreme Court   99
B. Federal Courts Relevant to North Carolina   99
1. United States District Courts   99
2. United States Courts of Appeals   99
3. United States Supreme Court   100

II. Publication of North Carolina Decisions   100

A. Official Reporters   101
    1. *North Carolina Reports*   101
    2. *North Carolina Court of Appeals Reports*   101
B. Unofficial Reporters   101
    1. *West's South Eastern Reporter*   101
    2. *North Carolina Cases*   102
C. Features of Reporters   102
    1. Advance Sheets   102
    2. Tables in Reporters   102
    3. Reporter Series   102
D. Online Fee-based Publication of North Carolina Cases   103
E. Online Free Publication of North Carolina Cases   104
    1. North Carolina Administrative Office of Courts Website   104
    2. North Carolina Cases from Other Websites   104
F. Parts of a Reported Case   105
G. Published vs. Unpublished   108

III. Publication of Other States' Judicial Opinions   108

IV. Publication of Federal Court Decisions   110
A. Print Publications   110
    1. Reporters for Federal Cases   110
        a. *Federal Supplement*   110
        b. *Federal Rules Decisions*   111
        c. *Federal Reporter*   111
        d. *Federal Appendix*   111
        e. *Federal Cases*   111
        f. *United States Reports*   111
        g. *United States Supreme Court Reports, Lawyers' Edition*   112
        h. *West's Supreme Court Reporter*   112
    2. Advance Sheets   112
B. Online Publication   112
C. Free Online Federal Cases   112
D. Published vs. Unpublished   113

V. Finding Cases Using Print Resources   113
A. Digests   114
    1. Headnotes   114
    2. Topics and Key Numbers, and Their Relationship
        to Headnotes   115
B. Methods of Using Digests   115

1. The "One Good Case" Method 117
2. Descriptive-Word Index Method 117
3. Topic Analysis or Outline Method 119
4. Table of Cases Method 119
5. Words and Phrases Method 120

VI. Finding Cases Online 120
A. West's Key Number Digest Online 120
    1. Initiating a Search using the West Key Number System 120
    2. Working from a Retrieved Case on the Screen 122
    3. Using a Topic and Key Number to Create a Search
      in a Database 122
B. Searching in WestlawNext's Practice Areas 122
C. Topic Searching on Lexis Advance 123
    1. "Browse Topics" Link above the Search Bar 123
    2. "Practice Areas and Topics" Link 123
    3. Working from a Retrieved Case on the Screen 124
D. Topic Searching in Bloomberg Law 125

Chapter 8 · Researching Administrative Rules and Decisions 127

I. North Carolina Administrative Law 128
A. Rules 128
    1. General Process of Creating Administrative Rules 128
    2. *North Carolina Administrative Code* 129
    3. *North Carolina Register* 130
B. Administrative Decisions 130

II. Researching North Carolina Administrative Rules 131
A. Starting with a Citation to a Rule from a Secondary Source 132
B. Starting with a Citation from an Authorizing or Enabling Statute 132
C. Browsing Titles in Print or Online 132
D. Searching the Index in Print 133
E. Searching the Administrative Code Online in Full Text or by
   Field or Segment 133
F. Using the *North Carolina Register* to Update 133

III. Researching North Carolina Administrative Decisions 134

IV. North Carolina Attorney General Opinions 134

V. Federal Administrative Law　　　　　　　　　　　　　　　135
  A. Administrative Regulations　　　　　　　　　　　　135
    1. *Code of Federal Regulations*　　　　　　　　　136
    2. *Federal Register*　　　　　　　　　　　　　137
    3. Researching Federal Administrative Regulations　　137
  B. Updating Administrative Regulations　　　　　　138
    1. Online　　　　　　　　　　　　　　　　　138
    2. Print　　　　　　　　　　　　　　　　　139
      a. *List of Sections Affected* Monthly Pamphlet　139
      b. *Federal Register* "CFR Parts Affected" Table　139
    3. Updating with Citators　　　　　　　　　　140
  C. Administrative Decisions　　　　　　　　　　　140

VI. Researching U.S. Attorney General Opinions　　　　　141

Chapter 9 · Updating Research　　　　　　　　　　143

I. Introduction　　　　　　　　　　　　　　　　　143
  A. Reasons for Updating　　　　　　　　　　　　143
  B. Citators　　　　　　　　　　　　　　　　　144

II. Updating Cases Using Shepard's on Lexis Advance　　145
  A. Accessing Shepard's　　　　　　　　　　　　145
    1. Shepardizing a Case Displayed on the Screen　145
    2. Shepardizing a Case Using the Citation　　146
  B. The Shepard's Display　　　　　　　　　　　146
  C. The Meaning and Use of the Citator Symbols　147
  D. Narrowing the Citing Documents　　　　　　148
  E. Analyzing the Citing Sources' Treatment of Your Case　149

III. Updating Cases Using KeyCite on WestlawNext　　150
  A. Accessing KeyCite　　　　　　　　　　　　150
  B. The KeyCite Display　　　　　　　　　　　150
  C. The Meaning and Use of the KeyCite Status Flags　152
  D. Limiting the Search Results　　　　　　　　153
  E. Analyzing the Citing Sources' Treatment of Your Case　154

IV. Updating Cases Using BCite on Bloomberg Law　154

V. Prioritizing Citing Sources　　　　　　　　　　156

VI. Updating Statutes　　　　　　　　　　　　　　157

A. Using KeyCite to Update Statutes   157
B. Using Shepard's on Lexis Advance to Update Statutes   158
C. Restricting Statutory Updates   158

VII. Updating Other Legal Information   158

Chapter 10 · Researching North Carolina Court Rules and
      Rules of Ethics   159

I. North Carolina Rules of Practice   159
  A. Rules of Procedure   159
    1. North Carolina Rules of Civil Procedure   160
    2. North Carolina Rules of Appellate Procedure 161
  B. Rules of Evidence   161
  C. Combined Sources of North Carolina Practice Rules   161

II. Federal Rules of Practice   162

III. North Carolina State Bar Rules, Rules of Ethics, and
   Ethics Opinions   163
  A. Rules and Regulations for the North Carolina State Bar 163
  B. 2003 Revised Rules of Professional Conduct   164
  C. Finding the Rules   165
  D. North Carolina Formal Ethics Opinions   165
  E. North Carolina Bar Association   166

IV. The American Bar Association and Legal Ethics   166

Epilogue · Revisiting the Research Process   167

I. Using a Research Process   167
  A. The Basic Process of Legal Research   167
  B. An Advanced Process of Legal Research   168

II. Knowing When to Stop   169

III. Keeping Perspective   170

Appendix A · North Carolina Routes of Appeal   171

Appendix B · Geographic Boundaries of the United States
      Judicial System   173

Appendix C · Legal Citation 175

I. North Carolina Citation Rules 176

II. Other States' Citation Rules 178

III. The *Bluebook* 179
  A. The *Bluebook*: Citations for Practice Documents 179
    1. Reference Guide and Bluepages 179
    2. Index 180
  B. Incorporating Citations into a Document 180
  C. Case Citations 181
    1. Essential Components of Case Citations 181
    2. Full and Short Citations to Cases 183
    3. Prior and Subsequent History 185
  D. Federal Statutes 185
  E. Signals 186
  F. Explanatory Parentheticals 187
  G. Quotations 187
  H. Citation Details 188
  I. The *Bluebook*: Citations for Law Review Articles 189

IV. *ALWD Citation Manual* 190

V. Editing Citations 191

About the Authors 193

Index 195

List of Tables and Figures

Tables

Table 1-1. Examples of Authority in North Carolina Legal Research   6

Table 2-1. Overview of the Basic Legal Research Process   11

Table 2-2. Generating Research Terms   14

Table 2-3. Examples of North Carolina Citations   19

Table 2-4. Fee-Based Services Providing Legal Information   23

Table 2-5. Selected Government Websites for North Carolina
Primary Legal Information   23

Table 2-6. Connectors and Commands for Keyword, Terms,
or Boolean Searching   26

Table 3-1. Outline for Selecting Appropriate Secondary Sources
for a Research Project   34

Table 3-2. Secondary Source Characteristics   35

Table 3-3. Examples of North Carolina Treatises   41

Table 3-4. Restatement Subjects   49

Table 3-5. Principles Subjects   49

Table 3-6. *North Carolina Pattern Jury Instructions*   53

Table 4-1. Articles of the North Carolina Constitution   56

Table 6-1. Documenting the North Carolina Legislative Process   79

Table 6-2. Process of Legislative History Research 86

Table 6-3. Comparison of Sources for North Carolina and
Federal Legislative History 96

Table 7-1. Online Providers of North Carolina Cases 103

Table 7-2. West's Regional Reporters and States Included 109

Table 7-3. Reporters for Federal Court Cases 110

Table 9-1. Symbols for Updating Cases with Shepard's 148

Table 9-2. KeyCite Depth of Treatment Symbols 152

Table 9-3. KeyCite Status Flags 152

Table 9-4. BCite Indicators 155

Table 10-1. North Carolina Revised Rules of Professional Conduct 164

Table E-1. Basic Legal Research Process 167

Table C-1. Purposes of Legal Citation 176

Table C-2. Example Judicial Citations under North Carolina Rules 177

Table C-3. North Carolina Court Designations When Only Citing
to Unofficial Reporters 178

Table C-4. Example North Carolina Statute and Rules Citations 178

Table C-5. Examples of Citation Sentences and Citation Clauses 181

Table C-6. Examples of Full Citations 184

Table C-7. Common Signals 186

Table C-8. *Bluebook* Typeface for Law Review Footnotes 189

Figures

Figure 3-1. Excerpt from *Strong's North Carolina Index* 37

Figure 6-1. Bill Report for House Bill 9/Session Law 2009-135 82

Figure 7-1. Example of a North Carolina Supreme Court Case
Viewed in *South Eastern Reporter* 105

Figure 7-2. Example of the Same North Carolina Supreme Court Case
Viewed in WestlawNext 106

Figure 7-3. Example from the *North Carolina Digest* 116

Figure 7-4. Browsing the List of Topics and Key Numbers
on WestlawNext 121

Figure 7-5. The Lexis Advance "Practice Areas and Topics" Page 124

Figure 7-6. The Lexis Advance Subtopics in Case Headnotes 125

Figure 7-7. The Health Practice Center Page in Bloomberg Law 126

Figure 9-1. Shepard's Citing Decisions Tab 147

Figure 9-2. KeyCite Tabs 151

Figure 9-3. KeyCite Filters 154

Figure E-1. Basic Legal Research Process 168

Series Note

The Legal Research Series published by Carolina Academic Press includes titles from states around the country as well as a separate text on federal legal research. The goal of each book is to provide law students, practitioners, paralegals, college students, laypeople, and librarians with the essential elements of legal research in each jurisdiction. Unlike more bibliographic texts, the Legal Research Series books seek to explain concisely both the sources of legal research and the process for conducting legal research effectively.

Preface and Acknowledgments

Many fine, nationally focused, legal research texts already exist. This book fills a unique niche by providing a North Carolina-focused, process-based, legal research textbook for law students and lawyers. As part of the state-specific Legal Research Series by Carolina Academic Press, this book is designed for use by new law students just learning how to engage in practical legal research in North Carolina. It could also be used as the basis for an advanced legal research course in North Carolina with additional supplementation from an instructor. Attorneys and laypeople alike might also find the book useful to reinforce their understanding of research with North Carolina legal information sources. The book's goal is to help students, attorneys, and laypeople all become savvy researchers.

North Carolina Legal Research uniquely focuses on a defined legal research process while incorporating specific North Carolina materials. Because few legal sources are published only online or only in print, the approach of the text is to assume format neutrality and complete integration of source formats. Due to circumstances beyond your control or due to personal preferences, you may not have access to all books or every premium online service. Throughout this book, an effort has been made to assume the use of either or both formats and descriptions of using either are included.

The book begins by laying a foundation for legal research and analysis, developing the idea of a research process and discussing some general strategies (Chapters 1 and 2). Next, the book follows a basic legal research process beginning with secondary sources in Chapter 3 and continuing with constitutional law, statutory law, case law, and administrative law (Chapters 4 through 8). The book finishes with chapters on updating the law, finding court rules and rules of ethics, and a last look at the process of legal research (Chapters 9 and 10 and the Epilogue). There are several supporting appendixes, most notably the final appendix addressing legal citation.

The primary change from the first edition is the emphasis on newer online platforms. While the first edition covered Westlaw Classic and Lexis.com, this edition addresses WestlawNext, Lexis Advance, and Bloomberg Law.

North Carolina Legal Research would not have been possible without the expertise of many people. The approaches taken in the other legal research books in this series were invaluable, and we appreciate the impact those authors' works had in shaping our ideas for this book. Most significantly, the series editor, Suzanne Rowe, invested her time and expertise in reviewing the manuscript and suggesting improvements. In addition to her valuable insights and important suggestions for each chapter, her legal citations appendix from *Oregon Legal Research* was the foundation for this book's legal citations appendix, which we adapted for use in North Carolina.

We remain in debt to those who helped with the first edition of this book, authored by Scott Childs. Patrick McCrary, UNC law student and research assistant, provided an important student perspective. UNC Law Library staff members Donna Nixon, Margaret Hall, Steve Melamut, Sandy Jones, and Denise Thompson provided priceless advice and assistance. Thanks are also due to the entire UNC Law Library staff for their understanding and patience throughout the length of this time-consuming project. Anne Klinefelter, UNC Law Library Director, provided amazing encouragement and support for the project as did the UNC School of Law administration. Finally, Hannah Choe, UNC law student and research assistant, and Jonathan Rountree, UNC reference librarian, provided invaluable support for the second edition.

North Carolina Legal Research

Chapter 1

Foundation for Legal Research and Analysis

I. North Carolina Legal Research

The basic process of researching the law is the same in most jurisdictions in the United States. Each jurisdiction, however, has its own nuances due to either unique legal structures or sources of law. Because of these nuances, a researcher must seek the specialized knowledge of the legal structures and sources of law in a jurisdiction before beginning the research process.

This book examines the process of legal research in the context of the specific structures and sources of law in North Carolina required to conduct efficient and effective legal research. Throughout the book, the examination of researching the law in North Carolina will be supplemented with brief discussions of researching federal law. On occasion, the ability to research federal law may be an important element of competently researching a legal issue arising in North Carolina. In a few instances, reference to researching the law of other states may be discussed for the purpose of highlighting differences.

II. The Role of Legal Analysis in Legal Research

This book promotes a process-centered approach to legal research. Although the book will discuss structures of the North Carolina legal system and the sources of law produced by that legal system, it will also address how the use of these sources fits into a broad process of researching. Once the legal research process is understood, the researcher may focus attention on the legal analysis that is required throughout the process.

Legal analysis drives the research process. What words will you use to search for law addressing the legal concepts you are researching? When you find primary law, how will you know what it means and how it applies to your issue or question? If you find a case that is relevant, how will you know whether law created after your case was decided changes how your case might be interpreted? These questions all involve legal analysis.

Legal analysis is the most challenging component of legal research, and it is particularly challenging for new law students or researchers unfamiliar with law. Law students will learn to engage in legal analysis throughout the three-year curriculum in law school. As your understanding of legal analysis deepens, the process of legal research will become both more logical and easier. For now, however, it is important to understand the sources of law and the basic process of legal research.

III. Types of Legal Authority

Researchers generally have a specific goal when conducting legal research. The goal might be to answer a specific question. A different goal might be to develop a broader understanding of a specific area of law. Whatever the goal might be, the researcher usually seeks information or a specific answer that is authoritative.

The concept of authority is important in legal research and analysis. To be useful, legal information must come from a person or organization authorized by the jurisdiction's constitution to say what the law is. In United States jurisdictions, in addition to constitutional provisions, researchers will be seeking statutory law from legislatures, judicial opinions from judges, and administrative rules or decisions from the executive branch. Preferably, the answer found will be issued from one or more of these authorized bodies within the geographic jurisdiction most relevant to the legal question being researched. However, there are different types of legal authority, which are applied in different ways.

A. Primary Authority

Primary authority is law issued by bodies constitutionally authorized to pronounce the law. The legislature adopts statutes requiring or prohibiting actions. The executive branch enforces these laws by promulgating detailed rules prescribing exactly how these statutes must be implemented and enforcing the laws. When legal disputes arise, judges hear arguments and issue decisions settling the disputes. All of these institutions are issuing primary law. In this manner, a body of primary law is created within a jurisdiction.

1. Mandatory Authority

Primary law of a jurisdiction is applied to legal issues that arise in that jurisdiction. For example, when a legal issue arises in North Carolina, a researcher seeks an answer from provisions of the North Carolina Constitution, statutes adopted by the North Carolina General Assembly, rules and decisions adopted by a North Carolina administrative agency, or cases issued by a North Carolina appellate court.

Primary law from the jurisdiction where a legal issue arises is called primary, mandatory authority. It is primary because of the body that issued it. It is mandatory because it was issued by institutions of the jurisdiction where the question arose and it is the law that must be applied. Most researchers seek primary, mandatory authority to address their question or the subject of their research. Primary, mandatory authority is binding within the jurisdiction in which it was issued.

2. Persuasive Authority

Primary authority that is issued by legislatures, courts, or administrative agencies from other state jurisdictions—outside of the jurisdiction where the legal issue being researched arose—is called primary, persuasive authority. This authority is primary because of the nature of the body issuing it, but only persuasive because it was not issued from a legal body of the relevant jurisdiction. While primary, persuasive authority is not mandatory outside of the jurisdiction in which it was issued, it might be persuasive when there is no existing primary, mandatory authority in a jurisdiction.

B. Secondary Authority

In contrast to primary authority issued by legal bodies within a jurisdiction, secondary authority is information about the law typically written by law professors, legal practitioners, or editors from legal publishers. This information may describe or explain the law, but it is not law itself. While there are levels of authoritativeness within the category of secondary authority, it is not the law. Therefore, secondary authority is always only persuasive, never mandatory. Notice this distinction in Table 1-1. As will be discussed in Chapter 3, secondary authority is an important source for finding and understanding primary law.

Table 1-1. Examples of Authority in North Carolina Legal Research

	Mandatory Authority	Persuasive Authority
Primary Authority	North Carolina Constitution	Virginia Constitution
	North Carolina General Statutes	South Carolina Code of Laws
	North Carolina Supreme Court Decisions	Georgia Supreme Court Decisions
Secondary Authority	___	Treatises
		Law Review Articles
		Legal Encyclopedias

C. Distinctions of Authority within Primary, Mandatory Authority

Within each jurisdiction, the constitution is the supreme law above all other primary law. Any law that is contrary to the constitution may be challenged and either overturned or reversed. A statute is next in the hierarchy of authoritativeness. Administrative rules issued by agencies are below statutes in the hierarchy. Judicial opinions often interpret statues or regulations, but cannot ignore those that are relevant. Judges may, however, determine that a statute violates the constitution or that an administrative rule reaches beyond its statutory authority.

It is only when there are no relevant constitutional provisions, statutes, or administrative rules on point that a question is determined by common law, often called case law. Although that might suggest that cases are less important in the research process, the importance of cases in legal research cannot be overstated. All other law in the hierarchy is often interpreted by judicial decisions when conflicts arise about the actual meaning of those other types of primary law. Therefore, a researcher may need to research case law even to determine the meaning of a provision of the constitution. Because of the importance of judicial decisions in legal research, the following section will focus on the court systems. This brief introduction is expanded in Chapter 7.

IV. Court Systems

In the typical court structure for most states and the federal judicial system in the United States, the trial court is the basic court where most legal issues are initiated and resolved. Often, more trivial or magisterial matters such as traffic violations or small claims matters may even be initiated below the trial court level. In addition to the basic trial courts, there are often specialized trial courts in many states, such as the North Carolina Business Court, which addresses complex business litigation. Other specialized courts might address family law or drug-related crimes where a court's particular subject expertise is important.

While the vast majority of litigation is concluded at the trial court level, most of the trial court decisions do not have precedential value because of the trial courts' low level in the court system hierarchy; therefore, these decisions not useful for research purposes. Trial court decisions are typically not widely published and often are not accompanied by written opinions. Limited reporting of trial court opinions occurs at the federal level and in very few state jurisdictions.

When researching case law, particularly in state jurisdictions, you will be researching appellate cases. In most state court systems as well as the federal court system, there is an intermediate appellate court, and an ultimate or supreme appellate court. The decisions of these courts are more important and more widely applicable than trial court decisions are. Appellate decisions are the focus of case law research.

A. North Carolina Courts[1]

In North Carolina, the trial court of general jurisdiction is the Superior Court. The Superior Court is divided into eight divisions and 50 districts across North Carolina's 100 counties. Ministerial matters, small claims, and some misdemeanor criminal cases are resolved at a lower level court below the Superior Court called the District Court. As in most states, these North Carolina trial courts typically do not publish their decisions, and their decisions do not have significant precedential value.

---

1. North Carolina courts are discussed more thoroughly in Chapter 7. For more information, see the North Carolina Court System homepage at www.nccourts.org. *See also* Scott Childs & Nick Sexton, *North Carolina Legal Research Guide* (2d ed., Hein Publ'g 2009).

From the Superior Court, an unhappy litigant may appeal to the North Carolina Court of Appeals, the intermediate appellate court in the state. Fifteen Court of Appeals judges sit in rotating panels of three to hear appeals from Superior and lower courts. One of the few exceptions is death penalty cases, which go directly to the North Carolina Supreme Court. At the Court of Appeals level and above, the focus of the appeal becomes errors of law or judicial interpretation. The appellate courts make no determinations of fact, but rather rely on the determinations made by the lower court.

The ultimate appellate court is the North Carolina Supreme Court. The Supreme Court is composed of a chief justice and six associate justices who hear cases together as a single panel. The Supreme Court may accept some cases on appeal by its discretion. The court also hears some appeals of right.

The North Carolina Court System webpage provides excellent information for researchers and practitioners alike.[2] In addition to descriptions of the courts and routes of appeals, the Court System website also provides current court calendars, rules and recent judicial appellate decisions. See Appendix A of this book, North Carolina Routes of Appeal, for a chart of the flow of appeals through the North Carolina court system.

B. Federal Courts

The federal judicial system is arranged much like the court system of North Carolina with a three-tiered design. The federal trial courts are called the United States District Courts. Some states only have one federal district, such as South Carolina, while other states contain several districts. North Carolina has three federal districts, the Western District, Middle District, and Eastern District. There are 94 total districts in the United States.

The federal intermediate appellate courts are called the United States Courts of Appeals. There are a total of thirteen federal circuits, each with a Court of Appeals. Eleven of those circuits are grouped together geographically by states. For example, North Carolina is in the Fourth Circuit, which also includes South Carolina, Virginia, West Virginia, and Maryland. The twelfth circuit is the United States Court of Appeals for the District of Columbia Circuit located in Washington, D.C. The thirteenth Court of Appeals was established in 1982 and is the United States Court of Appeals for the Federal Circuit. Unlike the

---

2. The page is maintained by the North Carolina Administrative Office of Courts and can be found at www.nccourts.org.

other Courts of Appeals, this court has appellate jurisdiction of certain limited subjects such as patent appeals.

The ultimate federal appellate court is the United States Supreme Court, which hears appeals from any of the thirteen federal Courts of Appeals or other specialized appellate courts. It also hears limited appeals from state supreme courts that involve issues of federal law.

In North Carolina, a litigant typically brings an action in federal district court in the appropriate federal district, Western, Middle, or Eastern. An appeal of that case would go to the United States Court of Appeals for the Fourth Circuit. The only appeal from the Court of Appeals for the Fourth Circuit would be to the United States Supreme Court. See Appendix B — Geographic Boundaries of the United States Judicial System, for a map of the federal judicial system.

C. Courts of Other States

With only minor differences, most other states share the same three-tiered judicial structure. Some states may split their intermediate appellate court into a civil and criminal branch, or may have a number of appellate courts, or may not have an intermediate appellate court at all. A few states call their ultimate appellate court something besides "supreme court"; however, the similarities among states are remarkable and facilitate the ease with which a researcher may engage in the process of legal research from one jurisdiction to another. In order to identify the specific court structure, names of the courts, and names of the official reporters of the courts' decisions for all state and federal courts, the researcher should consult a legal citation manual such as the *ALWD Guide to Legal Citation*[3] or the *Bluebook*.[4] For example, the *Bluebook*'s Table 1 has all of this information.

V. Organization of This Text

Chapter 2 will discuss the legal research process. The remainder of the text will follow the general flow of the basic legal research process from Table 2-1. Chapter 3 will address the use of secondary sources and their importance in the process of legal research. Constitutions, statutes, and legislative history

---

3. ALWD & Coleen Barger, *ALWD Guide to Legal Citation* (5th ed. 2014).

4. *The Bluebook: A Uniform System of Citation* (The Columbia Law Review Ass'n, et al. eds., 19th ed. 2010) ("*Bluebook.*)"

will be examined in Chapters 4, 5, and 6. While cases are critically important in our common law legal system, they do not appear until Chapter 7 because of their place in the research process. Chapter 8 introduces the concept of administrative law and the role it plays in legal research. No legal research project is complete without updating the information that has been found. The use of citators to update legal information is described in Chapter 9. How to research the important rules of ethics and rules of court is discussed in Chapter 10. Finally, the book will end with a quick look back at the research process.

Chapter 2

The Research Process: Strategies and Techniques

I. Overview of the Research Process

The goal of most legal research projects is to identify primary, mandatory authority that controls the legal issue being researched. Fortunately, there is a process to achieve that result. In addition to finding cases, statutes, and regulations, effective research often includes a quick review of commentary in the form of various secondary sources that provide background information and assist in understanding new or complex legal issues. The outline in Table 2-1 presents the basic research process.

Table 2-1. Overview of the Basic Legal Research Process

Step 1 Gather facts, identify the legal issues, determine the jurisdiction, and generate a list of search terms. Plan your research. Which sources will you use, in what order, and in what format? This chapter begins discussing these activities.

Step 2 Consult secondary sources such as legal encyclopedias, treatises, law journal articles, and practice materials for commentary providing background information as well as references to primary authority. Chapter 3 describes useful secondary sources and how they might be used in the research process.

Step 3 Find relevant statutes or constitutional provisions by searching for your research terms in statutory code indexes (either in print or online) or full-text searching a statutory code database. Read the relevant sections of statutes or constitutional provisions and begin thinking about how they apply to your research issue. Annotated statutory codes often provide useful references to additional sources of secondary and primary law, particularly cases. Chapters 4, 5, and 6 discuss sources of this kind of law and strategies for researching this information.

Step 4 Find relevant case law by using print digests (an arrangement of case law by subject for each jurisdiction) or online case-finding tools. Chapter 7 addresses finding and reading cases. Consider how the cases might clarify or complicate the law as it applies to your legal issue. Although research in Steps 2 and 3 is likely to lead to some cases, comprehensive research requires using the sources in Step 4.

Step 5 Find any relevant administrative rules or decisions. This is best done by browsing the annotations from a statutory code. Chapter 8 describes the sources of administrative law and strategies for finding it.

Step 6 Update the primary law you have located by using a citator such as Shepard's or KeyCite to ensure that the law you located has not been repealed, overruled, modified, or otherwise changed. The citing sources from the citators will also suggest how your case has been interpreted by subsequent authorities. Chapter 9 explains the use of citators to update information as well as to develop a greater understanding of how authority you have found has been understood and used in similar situations.

Step 7 If you have followed the research process, you will know that it's time to stop researching when you see the same authorities repeatedly cited throughout your research and there are no apparent gaps in your analysis. If you have used more than one method of searching for each research step, you can be more confident that you have found all of the relevant authorities.

The less you know about the area of law you are researching, the more useful it is to follow each step of the process. As you gain experience and knowledge, you can decide whether you are justified in skipping particular steps. For example, once you have researched a particular topic in a specific jurisdiction several times, you may feel confident that it is a topic that is not governed by administrative regulations and may skip Step 5. You must be certain, though, before you skip a step as failing to find relevant authorities can have serious consequences for you and your client.

After identifying the legal issues and the appropriate jurisdiction, the best starting point will almost always be secondary sources. The commentary found in those sources provides context and understanding of the issues to be researched as well as possible citations to relevant primary authority. In the future, as you learn more about the legal topic to be researched and the process of legal research itself, you might choose to adapt the process using the information you already know. For example, if you have gained a working knowledge of a legal topic and know that a specific question related to that topic is governed by statutory law, then you might choose to start your research with an annotated code, Step 3 in the process.

II. Planning a Research Strategy

A. Getting Started

1. Gathering Facts and Identifying Issues

The first step in the research process is to gather facts from the client or the person for whom you are researching. In the typical practice of law, this would involve interviewing a client and perhaps witnesses. Also consider reviewing relevant documents and speaking with colleagues or other professionals with relevant information or experience.

2. Determining Jurisdiction

One of the important first inquiries usually involves the determination of which jurisdiction's law applies to the issue. Is it a federal law issue or a state law issue? If it appears that the issue will be addressed by state law, which state? Where did the action occur? Who are the actors and where do they live? If both federal and state law may be applicable, how will they interact? The rules of civil or criminal procedure, and possibly other law, will determine the answers to these questions. The good news is that the basic research process outlined above is applicable in every jurisdiction. Note that you may need to research the jurisdictional issue before beginning to research the legal issue itself.

3. Generating Research Terms

Whether using online databases, print indexes, or digests to search for relevant law, you must begin by identifying the keywords or phrases that describe the issue being researched. These keywords are referred to as *research terms*. Knowing in advance whether you will be using online or print resources, or a combination of each, may lead to more efficient searching. The appendix at the end of this chapter explains why. In essence, print sources tend to be organized by controlled, standardized terms while the retrieval of online sources sometimes requires use of the exact language appearing in each relevant document.

Research terms may be generated in several ways. The traditional journalistic approach is to ask the questions: Who? What? When? Where? Why? and How? An alternative approach is to use TARPP, a mnemonic device that stands for Things, Actions, Remedies, People, and Places.

Consider the following example. A wife divorced her husband several years ago. Due to evidence regarding his lifestyle, his criminal past, the best interest of their child, and the totality of the circumstances, the court granted the mother custody and only limited visitation for the father. The father/ex-husband has made significant changes in his life and now approaches you as his attorney wanting to go back to court to gain joint custody of his child.

Depending upon your knowledge of family law, you might need to browse secondary sources before developing search terms. Alternatively, you might develop some basic search terms and then approach secondary sources to assist in refining them. Table 2-2 provides examples of research terms you might use to begin researching this project.

Table 2-2. Generating Research Terms

	Journalistic Approach
Who	child, children, mother, father, husband, wife, spouse, family
What	custody, child custody, modification, divorce, change in circumstances
When	post divorce, post custody order
Where	trial court, family court
How	modification, order, decree modification, motion
Why	change in circumstances, substantial change

	TARPP Approach
Things	custody, divorce, decree, circumstances
Actions	child custody modification, motion for modification, child custody order
Remedies	modification, order, decree modification
People	child, children, mother, father, husband, wife, spouse, family
Places	trial court, family court

Time invested in generating as many relevant search terms as possible is time well spent. From the initial list of terms, select the ones that appear most often or that seem connected. These may be among the most important. The list of search terms is dynamic throughout the research process. As the research progresses, new research terms will appear, particularly when you review secondary sources. Later in the process, as you read and evaluate the law in statutes or cases, you may need to add new terms to the list or remove existing terms from the list as your understanding of the issue and the law develops. You will begin to see how the issue is described and treated in the text of relevant documents such as cases, statutes, or regulations.

B. What Legal Information Do You Need?

Ideally, the process of legal research should be information driven, rather than format driven. Rather than initially deciding that you will only use books or you will only use Lexis, think instead about what information you anticipate needing. Once you have decided what information you need, you will be in a better position to identify the most efficient and effective source and format of that information. Although this is the ideal approach, outside of the academic environment your circumstances may limit your options. The library you are using may no longer subscribe to certain print series, or a particular client may be reluctant to pay online fees.

C. Choosing Between Print and Online Sources of Legal Information

In the modern research environment, researchers often have a choice of format when deciding where to search for relevant law or legal commentary to address the issue being researched. While traditional print publications are still available to some researchers, access to digital information from online vendors such as Westlaw, Lexis, and Bloomberg Law may increasingly be the format of choice for a growing number of purposes as interfaces improve. Lower-cost online vendors such as Loislaw, Fastcase, and Casemaker also provide access to smaller but substantial amounts of legal information. (Fastcase currently partners with the North Carolina Bar Association to provide free access to Bar Association members.) Additionally, the federal government and many state governments are now posting legal information on free government websites. Governments are beginning to develop ways of authenticating the digital information on their web pages, making it more reliable.

Confronted with an amazing array of sources of legal information that is growing every day, a savvy researcher gives careful consideration to the choice of format for legal information. The following seven considerations are some of the more important factors involved in making that decision. Each raises important questions for the researcher to answer. The seven considerations are intertwined with each other, and it's difficult to consider any one without involving one of the other factors.

1. Availability

While most traditional legal print sources of primary law are still being published, increasingly law libraries may not be purchasing this format due to cost or space issues. It is likely that some traditional print legal publications will cease being published in the near future as their costs rise and customers choose not to purchase them. The most recent primary law is available online either from fee-based online vendors or a free government website. While the editorial enhancements may vary widely from one online source to another, the text of the law should be consistent in all of these reputable sources. You will be better able to judge after reading this book the value of the editorial enhancements that are only available at a premium, from a few online sources.

Unlike primary law, authoritative secondary sources and other valuable commentary are less likely to be available for free online. When respected secondary sources or commentary are available online, they are often very expensive. The number of less authoritative legal commentaries on the Internet is growing. The price is right, but are they accurate and currently updated, and by whom?

2. Cost

The cost of a print publication is a one-time charge for ownership of the information, although the publication may require updating weekly, quarterly, or annually at a substantial cost. The benefit is that the purchaser may use the publication as often as desired without additional cost. How might the indirect cost of using this information be recaptured from the client?

Alternatively, online information may be priced in various ways. One pricing model is a *flat rate contract* for unlimited access to databases over a specific period of time. Or, an online service might have a *per-use access fee* so that the researcher is charged each time she accesses the database, which is more easily itemized for clients.

Other online pricing structures are possible, and much information is available for free. Many government organizations are posting law on government websites that are freely available. But if these sites are poorly organized, what is the cost of the additional time lost searching for the free information? If the information is not as currently updated as information from premium services, what is the cost of the additional time and effort required for more extensive updating? Also, what is the cost in time and efficiency of not having the editorial enhancements found in premium databases but lacking in free databases?

The role that cost plays in selecting the best format is complicated and very individualized. What is the value of your client's case or your research project? Do you have a client who is willing to pay a premium for costs incurred in researching the relevant law? In law practice, consider whether the financial value returned from your research offsets the expense invested in using high cost resources. If not, are there less expensive alternative sources of information that would lower the costs? Additional considerations involving cost might include what information your firm or organization has already purchased or what online licenses the firm has already entered into for access to legal information.

3. Accuracy

Researchers of all types have come to expect the information that they find to be accurate. This expectation may be due to the careful editing that permeates traditional print sources of legal information. Information found online may or may not have been carefully edited. Accuracy is always a concern, especially if the information provider is not an organization that traditionally edits information.

Accuracy is a particular concern for information so easily and freely accessible using the Internet. Sources such as Wikipedia are now widely used by many legal researchers including judges.[1] This is a period of transition concerning the accepted reliability of many digital sources, especially concerning those open source sites such as Wikipedia. The best practice for now is to always verify information from an unknown or less reputable source, including Wikipedia.

4. Age

Because law is constantly changing and evolving, the publication date of information can be critically important for researchers. Printed information is usually marked with a publication or copyright date. Printed supplements to books meant to update the contents are also typically dated. Online databases have the potential to be more current than print publications but are not always more current. Online information vendors often provide a "scope note" explaining how often a database is updated or perhaps providing the date last updated. Many researchers incorrectly assume a database is currently updated, simply because it is online. Researchers should always find the publication date for any information relied upon in the research process.

5. Context

The ability to see the broader picture is usually an important element of effective legal research. Information read out of context might be misinterpreted

---

1. *See* http://blogs.wsj.com/law/2012/04/23/which-federal-appeals-court-cites-wikipedia-most/.

or misunderstood. The ability to browse a table of contents and to view related text surrounding relevant information is critical. The need for context is particularly true when researching statutory or regulatory information, or commentary such as that found in legal treatises or encyclopedias. The nature of print publications facilitates this element. Online database services such as Westlaw, Lexis, and Bloomberg Law as well as state and federal government providers, are increasingly including top-level browsability as a display option.

6. Efficiencies

Efficiencies are typically very individualized to a specific researcher. For example, some researchers are more comfortable than others reading pages of text online. More objectively, however, print generally provides superior context, which might be more important early in the research process where the researcher's work is less focused and the researcher benefits from exposure to a wide array of information. Online research is more efficient when searching for a known document using specific information. Consider also the additional online efficiencies concerning the convenience of accessing information and either printing or downloading relevant documents.

7. Confidentiality

Attorneys are obligated to keep certain information private and may decide to keep other information confidential as a matter of strategy. Not all websites or online services guarantee the level of confidentiality needed in some circumstances. When using an online service, it is important to consider the privacy of your activity. This includes the safety of your device (such as a PC, laptop, or phone), the network (such as your office network or wireless Internet offered at a coffee shop), and the website itself. While the same information may be available on multiple online systems, each website or service may have different policies about what information is tracked, saved, and shared with third parties. Reviewing privacy policies and ensuring encrypted data transmission may be necessary when conducting sensitive legal research online.

D. Strategies for Research in Print Sources

Basic legal analysis has been intertwined with print sources of legal information for generations of lawyers and legal researchers. This connection was largely due to the West Digest System and the Topic and Key Number outline of American case law, first developed in the late 1800s. In order to locate cases, researchers had to analyze the legal issues within the framework of the digest system. Much value still remains in the digest system today, which explains why it is still available both in print as well as on Westlaw.

The following are selected strategies for using print resources, not just those published by West.

1. Using Known Citations or Names to Locate Specific Documents

a. Using Citations to Specific Publications

Retrieving a document with a known citation is the easiest approach to finding information in print (or online for that matter). You may know a *citation* because the assigning associate gave you a citation or your previous research identified citations for you to retrieve. The general three-part nomenclature for a legal citation is the volume number, abbreviation of the title of the source, and the page or section number within that volume where the relevant document may be found. See Table 2-3 for examples of citations from North Carolina.

Table 2-3. Examples of North Carolina Citations

Type of Information	Source	Cases, Citation
Judicial Opinion	North Carolina Supreme Court	*Smith v. Jones*, 76 N.C. 125 (2009)
	North Carolina Court of Appeals	*Hewes v. Johnston*, 61 N.C. App. 603 (1983)
Statutory Code (North Carolina General Statutes)	North Carolina General Assembly	N.C. Gen. Stat. § 150B-36
Law Review Articles	North Carolina Law Review	45 N.C. L. Rev. 135
Treatises	Published by LexisNexis Matthew Bender	*Brandis and Broun on North Carolina Evidence* (7th ed. 2011)

b. Using the Proper Name of a Litigant or an Act

Occasionally, you might be given the name of a party in a case as a reference to assist in finding that case. The West Digest System in each jurisdiction includes volumes with an alphabetical listing of cases by party name. The list includes a citation to the specific reporter where each case may be found. Likewise, you might take the popular name of a legislative act to the popular name table that is part of each jurisdiction's statutory code and find a specific citation to the act.

2. Browsing Tables of Contents

At the beginning of most books or digests is a *table of contents* explaining how information in that publication is divided and where specific information might be found inside. Scanning the table of contents for relevant search terms is a quick way of locating the information, especially when using broader search terms. The table of contents may provide references to page numbers, section numbers, or paragraph numbers. The other important role for tables of contents in legal research is the opportunity to see relevant information in relation to the other similar information in the publication. Seeing this analytical overview informs the researcher of potentially relevant information not yet identified or confirms the appropriateness of the information being sought.

For example, scanning the table of contents of a "topic" in a case law digest provides an opportunity for additional legal analysis where the researcher can review all of the potentially relevant subtopics within that topic. Scanning a legal encyclopedia's table of contents provides the same opportunity to see the broader view of the subject you are researching.

3. Browsing an Index for a Specific Legal Term

The more obvious approach to print sources of law is to browse the index for your search terms. The *index* provides specific places in the text where the terms appear, referenced by page number, section number, or paragraph number. The index is typically located at the end of a publication, whether a single-volume or multiple-volume publication.

Indexes are more specific than tables of contents. Rather than providing an overview of a publication's content, the index is an alphabetical list of all the important terms in the publication. Because it is specific and detailed, an index typically includes some related terms that are similar to, but not necessarily found in, those terms in the documents. These cross-references direct the researcher from her own search terms to the indexed search terms from the document; the indexed terms will lead her to the document.

4. Browsing Pocket Parts and Supplements to Update

Hardbound, law-related books are in constant need of updating. Most bound, legal publications are updated with *pocket parts*. These are periodic supplements (usually published annually) that are placed in a back pocket of each volume of a publication. Pocket parts may be found in single-volume books or multi-volume series, where each volume should have a pocket part. The importance of reviewing the pocket part cannot be overstated. Whatever material was reviewed in the main text should also be reviewed in the pocket part to determine whether there are any changes in the law affecting this subject. If a pocket part becomes too large to fit within the cover of a volume, a free-standing pamphlet version of the pocket part is published to be shelved beside the hardbound volume. It is used in the same manner. Pocket parts or pamphlets will contain the most recent information available in print. Note that many secondary resources that are available online may only be as current as the most recent paper pocket part or pamphlet for that title.

Occasionally, a set of books may have a free-standing pamphlet instead of or in addition to pocket parts. For example, *West's North Carolina General Statutes Annotated* is updated both by annual pocket parts as well as by quarterly or semi-annual pamphlets. Likewise, the *United States Code Annotated* is updated with annual pocket parts and quarterly pamphlets.

E. Strategies for Research in Online Sources

The use of online resources is critically important when conducting efficient and effective legal research in today's environment. The following explanation of basic online research strategies lays the foundation for understanding discussions of researching specific types of legal information in later chapters.

1. Overview of Commercial Research Services

The three largest and most comprehensive commercial providers of online legal information are Westlaw, Lexis, and Bloomberg Law. Two of those services, Westlaw and Lexis, have been serving the legal community for decades, greatly expanding access to legal information and evolving over the years with the changing technology. Bloomberg Law is a newcomer to the legal information field, but has developed an impressive array of features and content.

Westlaw is owned by Thomson Reuters and provides nearly comprehensive access to legal information. Periodically the Westlaw search engine and interface change due to technological advances. As of the writing of this book, WestlawNext is the most recent version of the Westlaw research product. Released in 2010, WestlawNext presents a universal search bar in which you may enter keywords, natural language-type phrases, or known citations. Importantly, the site provides substantial browsability, enabling a more sophisticated researcher to select specific databases within which to browse or search. Whenever this book discusses how to access information from Westlaw, the discussion will focus exclusively on the WestlawNext product.

Lexis is a Reed Elsevier product, also providing nearly comprehensive access to legal information. The most recent version of the Lexis research product is Lexis Advance, released in 2011. Like WestlawNext, Lexis Advance presents a universal search bar in which you may enter keywords, natural language-type phrases, or known citations. Although Lexis Advance currently provides less browsability than WestlawNext does, changes are slated later this year that will expand that capability and facilitate more sophisticated and directed searching. This book's discussion of Lexis will focus exclusively on the Lexis Advance product.

Bloomberg Law is a 2010 product of Bloomberg L.P., a publisher long known and respected for company and market information and related news. Bloomberg Law acquired Bureau of National Affairs (BNA) in 2011. Bloomberg's ability to provide sophisticated and comprehensive legal news as well as an array of commentary, analysis, and primary law was greatly enhanced through the BNA products. Like WestlawNext and Lexis Advance, the Bloomberg Law interface also presents a single search bar for instant searching with keywords; however, it currently does not support natural language searching.

Although distinctions exist between the services, Westlaw and Lexis products each approach near comprehensiveness in content and share many common strategies for efficient use. While Bloomberg Law may lack in overall comprehensiveness, it excels at providing extensive litigation and transactional resources, including superior court tracking capability, as well as excellent access to current legal news and legal current awareness resources.

Generally, the explanations of online search strategies in this section apply specifically to those three services. Major differences will be identified. Although prices vary depending upon specific uses, these three services are relatively expensive. A growing number of less expensive fee-based alternatives exist, generally providing primary legal information with substantially fewer editorial enhancements and secondary sources of legal information. There are also some government websites providing free access to basic and recent primary law. Table 2-4 provides examples of leading fee-based, online legal information providers. Table 2-5 lists examples of free North Carolina government websites for legal information.

Table 2-4. Fee-Based Services Providing Legal Information

Bloomberg Law	bloomberglaw.com/
Fastcase	www.fastcase.com (free to North Carolina Bar Association members)
Lexis	www.lexis.com
Loislaw	www.loislaw.com
VersusLaw	www.versuslaw.com
Westlaw	www.westlaw.com

Table 2-5. Selected Government Websites
for North Carolina Primary Legal Information

North Carolina Constitution

www.ncleg.net/Legislation/constitution/ncconstitution.html

North Carolina Statutes

www.ncga.state.nc.us/gascripts/statutes/Statutes.asp

North Carolina Cases

appellate.nccourts.org/opinions/

North Carolina Administrative Law

www.oah.state.nc.us

2. Using Known Citations to Locate Specific Documents

You may conveniently retrieve a document on Westlaw, Lexis, or Bloomberg Law by entering a known *citation*—typically including a volume number, a publication abbreviation, and a page number—into the universal search bar. This feature is effective for retrieving cases, journal articles, statutory provisions, and administrative code sections for example. The correct citation formats for North Carolina (and other jurisdictions) are available in the two standard citation guides for law, *The Bluebook: A Uniform System of Citation*,[2] and the *ALWD Guide to Legal Citation*.[3]

---

2. The *Bluebook* is compiled by the editors of the Columbia Law Review, the Harvard Law Review, the University of Pennsylvania Law Review, and the Yale Law Journal. The *Bluebook* is published and distributed by the Harvard Law Review Association. *See* www.legalbluebook.com.

3. The fifth edition of the *ALWD Guide* is written by Coleen Barger and the Association of Legal Writing Directors. *See* http://www.alwd.org/publications/citation-manual/.

3. Browsing Online by Topic

One of the great improvements in the last decade in researching with online information is the increasing availability of browsing online. Online browsability adds the advantage of context in searching that is common in print publications. Several online browsing options include the following.

a. Browsing on WestlawNext

WestlawNext provides an easily accessible browsing window in the center of the page, just below the universal search bar at the top. The window provides options for browsing the 25 law-related categories under "All Content," browsing by state or federal jurisdiction, browsing by 26 legal topics, or browsing a short list of tools.

b. Browsing on Lexis Advance

Lexis Advance currently provides less browsing access to resources. From the main page, just above the universal search bar, you may select "Browse Topics" and select from 43 law-related topics. You may also select "Browse Sources," which allows you to browse or search for a specific title or source of information. The "Browse Sources" option allows you to also narrow or filter your results by content type or jurisdiction.

c. Key Number Digest of Case Law on WestlawNext

Over 400 topics, subdivided into thousands of subtopics are available on Westlaw. This is the currently updated contents of the entire West Digest System developed over 100 years ago, available online. Browsing the digest is a complex task for new researchers and will be more fully discussed in Chapter 7.

d. Tables of Contents of Specific Sources

A number of publications available on WestlawNext, Lexis Advance, and Bloomberg Law are available in a table of contents format where you may select a topic and be presented with a sub-menu of topics. Titles include the *General Statutes of North Carolina*, several encyclopedias (not currently available on Bloomberg), and a number of treatises or books about the law. The initial table of contents is typically presented at a relatively generalized level, accompanied by plus signs adjacent to the headings. Clicking on the plus symbol expands the information to the layer of more specific subheadings below. Usually, these layered menus eventually lead to the actual text of a document, or in some cases, a search box for a specific, focused part of the database. This feature is also available for free on some North Carolina government-sponsored legal information websites. For example, *North Carolina General Statutes* at the General Assembly website is browsable in this fashion.

4. Keyword Searching

a. Methods and Strategies for Full-text Keyword Searching

Keyword searching, sometimes called *terms and connectors* (or *Boolean logic*) searching, allows the most control over an online search. Generally, West-lawNext and Lexis Advance will perform terms and connectors or Boolean searching if you enter terms with connectors. Otherwise, those services will default to natural language searching with the search terms you enter. Bloomberg Law will only perform terms and connector searching and does not provide natural language searching at this time. Natural language searching is discussed below in Section 5 of this chapter.

Using the terms and connector or the Boolean searching method, you first identify search terms as previously discussed in Chapter 1. When searching full-text, it's important to think of all the various ways your terms might have been described by the authors of every document in the database you search. For example, in a case law database, there are many individual authors (judges) of the cases in the database. What language did each of them use to describe your search terms? The fewer the possibilities there are, the more likely you are to retrieve all of the relevant documents.

After identifying search terms, you next define the relationships between the search terms using connectors. A basic understanding of how the connectors can be used is essential to effective searching. Table 2-6 summarizes the most common connectors used with WestlawNext, Lexis Advance, and Bloomberg Law.

As demonstrated in Table 2-6, the use of the connectors is predominantly the same for WestlawNext, Lexis Advance, and Bloomberg Law. Several points should be highlighted.

Phrase searching is a particularly specific method of searching, especially when the phrase is a term of art or a search term most likely to appear in all relevant documents. All of the services require the words in a phrase to be included within quotation marks to be searched as a phrase using the Boolean search method.

In addition to the relationship established between two terms by each connector, there is a default order in which two or more connectors are processed in each search. The order in which connectors are processed may greatly affect the outcome of the search. The general default order of processing follows this sequence: "phrase," OR, W/N, W/S, W/P, AND, But Not (And Not).

Table 2-6. Connectors and Commands for Keyword, Terms, or Boolean Searching

Goal	Lexis Advance	WestlawNext	Bloomberg Law
Find either term anywhere in the document	Or	Or	Or
Find both terms anywhere in the document	And &	And &	And
Find both terms within a particular distance from each other	w/p = both terms within 1 paragraph w/s = both terms within 1 sentence w/n = both terms within n words	/p = both terms within 1 paragraph /s = both terms within 1 sentence /n = both terms within n words	/p = both terms within 1 paragraph /s = both terms within 1 sentence /n = both terms within n words
Find terms used as a phrase	Put the phrase in quotation marks	Put the phrase in quotation marks	Put the phrase in quotation marks
Control the order of Boolean searching	Parentheses ( )	Parentheses ( )	Parentheses ( )
Exclude terms	And not	But not %	Not And not But not
Extend the end of a term (root expander)	Exclamation point ! Example: run!	Exclamation point ! Example: run!	Exclamation point ! Example: run!
Hold the place of letters in a term for all alternative letters	Asterisks * Example: wom*n	Asterisks * Example: wom*n	Asterisks * Example: wom*n

EXAMPLE: apartment w/3 lease and pets or dogs

Since the "or" connector is processed first in this search, the system would begin by locating documents with either "pets" or "dogs" anywhere in the text.

Next, the system would locate documents where "apartment" is found within three words of "lease."

Finally, the system would combine the requirements to retrieve only those documents that contained either "pets" or "dogs" as long as "apartment" was within three words of "lease" in each document.

You may change this default order of processing by placing parentheses around the parts of your search that you want processed first. Terms and connectors within parentheses will be processed first—in the default order listed above—and then the terms and connectors outside of the parentheses will be processed.

EXAMPLE: (apartment w/3 lease and pets) or dogs

Within the parentheses, the system would begin by searching for documents containing "apartment" within three words of "lease."

Next, the system would limit that set of documents to just those that also contained the word "pets" somewhere in the document.

Finally, the system would also retrieve all cases containing the word "dogs."

As you can see, placement of the parentheses could produce dramatically different results from the default order of processing. Placement of the parentheses can be used to significantly alter your search.

A common online search strategy is to begin your search in the smallest database that you know will contain all the relevant documents. For example, if you are searching for North Carolina cases, select a database that has only North Carolina cases rather than one including cases from all fifty states. Initiate a broad, inclusive search, once you have selected the smallest database you believe will contain all of the relevant documents.

After formulating and running a search, you must evaluate the results that the search retrieves. Typically, you should contemplate additional refining based upon the effectiveness of the search and incorporating what you learned in the initial search. For this initial broad-search approach, WestlawNext, Lexis Advance, and Bloomberg Law all have a feature allowing you to filter the initial retrieved set of documents by jurisdiction, source or type of information, etc., depending upon the contents of the database. Look for these options when viewing a retrieved set of search results. These types of filters may have the additional benefit of often being "free" for those customers paying transactional costs or using per-search pricing.

b. Keyword Searching an Online Index Database

For a few large databases of information where a print index already exists, WestlawNext and Lexis Advance provide a separate database containing just the index that may be searched or browsed. This feature brings the advantage of a human-analyzed set of search terms identified from within the database and associated with their locations within each document. The index databases may include a search engine or simply be a browsable list of all the index terms as would be found in the print index. Using the index database might be an excellent way to approach a code of statutory law, such as the *North Carolina General Statutes* rather than using a full-text keyword search of the entire code database. Bloomberg Law currently provides fewer opportunities for index searching.

c. Keyword Searching a Field or Segment of Each Document in a Database

Field searching is a feature allowing researchers to limit their search to just certain parts of each document in a database rather than searching each word of every document. For example, if you are trying to find a particular case in a database and have a plaintiff's name, you can search just the part of all the cases in the database that includes the plaintiff's name. Field searching might also be an effective search strategy to use when trying to locate all the decisions written by a particular judge. You could limit your search to just the "judge" field of each case in the database and use the judge's name as the search term. By limiting the search to just that field, you would not retrieve cases that mention this judge's name in the text, only those actually authored by the judge.

Field searching is usually only available on the more expensive online services and is less common in free databases on government websites. WestlawNext provides this option using the "advanced" link, just beside the universal search bar. Bloomberg Law provides this option at the bottom of the typical search screen; it can usually be found by simply scrolling down the screen. Lexis Advance achieves a similar result by allowing extensive filtering of these same fields whose content is populated by the initial search.

5. Natural Language Searching

Natural language searching allows you to enter search terms without connectors. You may even enter an English language sentence stating the question being researched. The system's software uses predetermined calculations or algorithms to determine which words in your search are the most important and which documents in the database are most relevant to your terms. While you have little control over the search, sometimes this approach may be useful if you are having difficulty retrieving relevant documents with a keyword search. Also, retrieved documents are automatically ranked by relevancy in a natural language search. Documents retrieved in a keyword search are automatically presented in reverse chronological order, with the most recent documents presented first. At the present, Bloomberg Law only provides the more sophisticated terms and connectors or Boolean searching, and does not support natural language searching.

III. Interconnectedness of Legal Information

An important element in legal research is the concept of the interconnectedness of the information. This interconnectivity manifests itself in several ways and facilitates an easier legal research process.

First, there are several sources that are outstanding "connectors" of different types of related legal information. Annotated codes, for example, connect statutory law with case law, administrative law, and law review articles through the annotations associated with each code section. By integrating an annotated code early in your research process, you benefit more from the annotations. For this reason, annotated codes are often the first primary law source to approach after starting your search in secondary sources. Annotated codes will be discussed more in Chapter 5.

An outstanding secondary source providing excellent interconnectivity is *American Law Reports* (ALR). An ALR annotation can provide a wealth of information leading to relevant cases, statutes, and other secondary sources. While other secondary sources are excellent in their own ways and for particular purposes, ALR annotations are excellent sources for connecting you with important, related primary and secondary information. *American Law Reports* will be discussed in great detail in Chapter 3.

Another way that legal information is interconnected is through various formats produced by the same publisher. Most famously interconnected is the West Digest Topic and Key Number System, which is available in print and on

WestlawNext. You may easily move from a Topic and Key Number in the print digest onto WestlawNext to locate cases classified under that heading. Chapter 7 will address this search tool in greater detail. For now, understand that you may research seamlessly from WestlawNext to West print digests and back to WestlawNext without losing time or energy in the transition.

The savvy researcher grasps the interconnectivity and takes advantage of it for convenience and efficiency. Look for other ways in which legal information is interconnected as you progress through the book.

IV. Organizing and Modifying the Research Process

Following the basic process of legal research, as outlined in Table 2-1, is an excellent way of staying organized. While you will undoubtedly go off on tangents to research specific sub-issues that arise, by following the process described in this chapter you will be assured of searching for all relevant types of law and related legal information. Each individual has a unique method of organizing within this process. The important elements are to know where you are in the process and take good notes in case you need to replicate any of your research.

Even the strictest organizers will find that research becomes tangled. The leading contributor to the tangle is the need to modify your research focus throughout the process. As your research moves forward and you learn new things about your legal issue, you will also need to amend your search terms and may need to narrow or expand your research. This clarification process will be addressed again at the end of the book.

Appendix

The Difference Between Search Terms for Indexes and Digests vs. Search Terms for Online Searching

Indexes and digests are typically created by human beings reading law and classifying it by subject using standard language or standard subject areas. The text of the law itself might not include the actual index or digest terms under which the law is classified. For example, the West digest system of cases assigns specific topics and subtopics to each area of law. When using indexes or digests, you must develop research terms matching the standard language by which law is indexed in the particular digest. The advantage is that once you identify the standard language used by the index or digest, you will find a relatively comprehensive list of citations to the relevant law.

Attorneys have used the West digest system for over 100 years. Many experienced attorneys still practicing law will comfortably analyze legal issues in terms associated with the West Digest System. The more familiar you are with the standard language of those digest topics and subtopics, the more likely your search in the digest will be efficient and successful. The difficulty of using a digest or index is determining the "standard" language the indexer used to describe the legal issue.

Alternatively, when you use research terms in a full-text database of cases posted by your State's court, for example, you are trying to think of every possible way that your legal issue or relevant facts might have been expressed by the authors of the documents you seek. For example, when searching case law you should think of every way that each judge writing a relevant opinion addressing your legal issue would have described the issue. If a judge writing a relevant opinion described and discussed your legal issue in different terms than the precise terms you select as your research terms, your online search will not retrieve that relevant case. The lack of a controlled vocabulary usually makes the certainty of finding all the relevant cases and only the relevant cases more difficult. In full-text online searching, a tension always exists between finding all of the relevant cases and finding only the relevant cases.

By considering the differences in these two methods, you can see why it matters when selecting search terms that you know whether you will be using an index or whether you will be searching a full-text database. Each of these two approaches has strengths and weaknesses, and no single approach will always be the best approach. The approaches may even produce different results. You may need to conduct both kinds of searches to find all relevant cases. In addition, some premium services have taken steps to ameliorate some of the online searching weaknesses. For example, WestlawNext includes the standardized language from the digest in the case headnotes for cases in their case law databases. Also, the WestlawNext search engine may include additional related terms even if you did not include those terms as part of your search. These search enhancements are typically not available in the lower-cost and free online databases of case law.

Chapter 3

Researching Secondary Sources

I. Introduction

Various law professors, legal experts, editorial staff of legal publishing companies, and many organizations produce commentary about the law. This commentary is considered to be secondary to the law itself. Although there are levels of authoritativeness among secondary sources, none of these sources provides mandatory authority that must be followed by any jurisdiction. However, secondary sources are an important component in the process of finding and understanding primary law.

A. The Role of Secondary Sources in the Legal Research Process

The savvy researcher quickly learns how to use secondary sources in most any legal research project. Secondary sources provide an excellent starting point for research, whether using print or online sources. A few minutes spent reviewing an appropriate secondary source at the beginning of the project provides various levels of background information that efficiently enhances understanding of the legal issues involved in a research project. This understanding greatly improves the research process by (1) enabling the researcher to select more relevant research terms when searching databases, indexes, or digests; (2) providing direct citations to relevant mandatory authority; and (3) facilitating a faster, deeper, and more efficient recognition and understanding of the primary law retrieved in the research process.

Although the basic legal research process introduced in Chapter 2 appears to be linear, a researcher may need to review secondary sources throughout the research process to either refocus or broaden her understanding of the primary law issues being researched. Because law is interdependent and often cannot effectively be interpreted in a narrow context, a detailed yet broad understanding of legal issues is typically required. Secondary sources may conveniently serve either of these purposes: delving deeply into a specific legal topic (or even a narrow subtopic) or broadly surveying an area of law for an understanding of a legal topic as a whole or how the legal topic is interpreted in relation to other legal topics.

B. Secondary Sources and Practice Materials

Legal encyclopedias, legal treatises, law reviews or journals, *American Law Reports* annotations, and Restatements of the Law are the five traditional secondary sources of law. Each of these sources provides a unique view of law and may have different purposes throughout the research process. These five secondary sources will be addressed in turn to begin this chapter. Many, many other secondary sources of law might be categorized as practice materials; they are covered at the end of the chapter. These materials might include recent materials from continuing legal education programs, legal forms (e.g., examples of motions and complaints), model jury instructions, uniform laws, and law-related blogs.

C. Selecting the Most Relevant Secondary Source

Secondary sources have different strengths and weaknesses and can be used in different ways while researching. If you understand those strengths and weaknesses, you will be able to select the most useful secondary source for your research project. Researchers are typically working under time constraints and do not have time to review an extensive list of secondary materials. Rather, 20 or 30 minutes spent browsing one or two carefully selected sources can pay dividends in time and understanding. See Table 3-1 for an outline of selecting appropriate secondary sources for a research project. Table 3-2 summarizes the strengths and weaknesses of the five traditional secondary sources.

Table 3-1. Outline for Selecting Appropriate Secondary Sources for a Research Project

1. Determine what you are trying to accomplish with your research. Are you searching for a quick, broad overview of a legal topic or a deep but narrowly focused description of a discrete area of law? Do you need criticism and analysis of existing law? Do you need recommendations for changes in the law?

2. Examine the chart in Table 3-2 explaining the strengths and weaknesses of the five traditional secondary sources.

3. Match the purpose of your research with one or two secondary sources having strengths in areas addressing your research goal. For example, a legal encyclopedia will provide a broad, descriptive overview of a legal topic. An *American Law Report* annotation will drill down deep into a narrow topic, providing description and citations to primary law, but will provide no criticism or analysis.

Table 3-2. Secondary Source Characteristics

	Arrangement: Topic, Serial, Alphabetical	Current Topic Coverage	Depth of Coverage	Description &/or Commentary	Reputation of the Author	Updating: Frequency & Means
Restatements	Published separately by topic, such as torts or contracts.	Least current. The law evolves more rapidly than Restatements are written.	Great depth of coverage of topics, with examples and commentary.	Describes what the law is. Includes examples and notes.	Highest—could cite these in court as persuasive but never mandatory.	Case citations are updated, but text is rarely updated.
Treatises	Published separately by topic. Available for nearly every legal topic.	Effort to stay current—but maybe less than periodicals or ALRs.	Broad, well organized coverage, usually with good depth.	Primarily describes the law but may also offer commentary and critique.	High—depending on the individual author.	Depends—usually annually but could be more or less frequently.
Periodicals (Law reviews and law journals)	Serially published, not by topic. Must use index or keyword.	Most current, along with ALRs.	Usually very deep.	Could be either description of the law, or critique of the law, or both. Many references.	Can be persuasive but only if highly reputable author.	Updated only by publication of new articles.
ALR Annotations	Serially published, not by topic. Must use index or keyword.	Most current, along with periodicals.	Very deep analysis, but very narrow focus.	Description of what the law is and comparative analysis but no commentary. Many references.	Attorney-authored articles—slightly better than encyclopedias.	New annotations serially & annual case citation updates.
Legal Encyclopedia	Alphabetical publication. Must use index or keyword.	Poor—only slightly better than Restatements.	Broadest single tool, but generally not very deep.	Description only.	Usually editor-authored but could be signed—least authoritative.	Slow—annual pocket parts—mostly case updates.

D. Online vs. Print

Many researchers find that, when using secondary sources, being able to quickly browse and view related content is important because it provides the context in which to understand information efficiently. Some researchers find print sources are superior in providing context. However, online vendors have recently improved the presentation of secondary sources to include browsable tables of contents and other helpful features typically found in print. Whichever format you choose, look for how the information you seek fits in the larger context for a more comprehensive understanding of the issues.

II. Legal Encyclopedias

Legal encyclopedias are one of the most basic of the secondary sources and, if available, are often most useful as a beginning point for legal research. The information is organized into topics that are alphabetically arranged in multiple volumes. Encyclopedias typically provide broad coverage, which assists in determining which area or areas of law might control your legal issue. *Strong's North Carolina Index* is a publication that functions as a North Carolina encyclopedia, although it might be slightly less descriptive than other typical state legal encyclopedias. The two main national legal encyclopedias are *American Jurisprudence* and *Corpus Juris Secundum*.

A. *Strong's North Carolina Index*

Strong's North Carolina Index is a 50-plus volume encyclopedic treatment of North Carolina law, currently in its fourth edition. Like most legal encyclopedias, *Strong's* describes the law generally without commentary and provides citations to North Carolina cases as well as citations to relevant provisions of the North Carolina Constitution, *North Carolina General Statutes*, court rules, and occasional journal articles. Additionally, there is a 12-volume "archived" edition of *Strong's* containing older case law. This is a separate, print publication that is often shelved in libraries near the main set. See Figure 3-1 for an excerpt from *Strong's North Carolina Index.*

1. Researching with Print

Begin researching in *Strong's* by using the Descriptive-Word Index at the end of the print set. References should be made to sections within the main set that refer to your search terms. *Strong's* also provides a Table of Cases so

Figure 3-1. Excerpt from *Strong's North Carolina Index*

NCINDEX ADVERSE § 24
§ 24 Possession under color of title; seven years
Approx. 1 page

FOR EDUCATIONAL USE ONLY
1 N.C. Index 4th Adverse Possession § 24

Strong's North Carolina Index 4th
Database updated August 2009

Adverse Possession
Elizabeth Williams, J.D.

I. Requisites of Adverse Possession
B. Period of Possession
1. Statutory Periods To Ripen Title

Topic Summary   Correlation Table

§ 24. Possession under color of title; seven years

National Background: As to adverse possession under color of title, generally, see 3. Am. Jur. 2d. Adverse Possession §§ 143–149; C.J.S. Adverse Possession §§ 88–105.

Statutes:

When a person or those under whom the person claims is and has been in possession of any real property, under known and visible lines and boundaries and under color of title, for seven years, no entry may be made of action sustained against such possessor by a person having any right or title to the same, except during the seven years next after his right or title has descended or accrued, who in default of suing within that time will be excluded from any claim thereafter made; and such possession, so held, is a perpetual bar against all persons not under disability. Commissioners' deeds in judicial sales and trustees' deeds under foreclosure also constitute color of title.[FN46]

Cases:

In actions between individual litigants where the claimant has color of title to disputed real property, adverse possession for seven years is necessary to ripen title to the property in the claimant.[FN47]

[FN46] GS § 1-38(a).
For discussion of the period needed to ripen title in state lands under color of title, see § 26.
As to what constitutes color of title, generally, see §§ 10 et seq.
As to known and visible lines and boundaries, see § 6.

Source: Reprinted with permission of Thomson-Reuters.

that you may approach the set with a case name and locate a discussion of that case in *Strong's*. Finally, the set includes a Words and Phrases index with an alphabetical list of specific phrases or words that have been judicially defined and citations to the cases where the definitions appear. Each volume of *Strong's* is updated with annual pocket parts, and the set is also updated with quarterly pamphlets.

2. Researching with Strong's on Westlaw

Strong's is also contained in a database on WestlawNext and may be found by entering "Strong's North Carolina Index" in the universal search bar. The database on WestlawNext may be browsed using a table of contents approach or the full text may be searched using keywords (terms and connectors) or natural language. The Strong's database also incorporates the contents of the separately published "archived" edition. The database appears to be updated at least quarterly.

B. *American Jurisprudence, 2d*

American Jurisprudence, 2d (Am Jur) is a broad, encyclopedic treatment of American law covering state and federal law, civil and criminal law, and procedural and substantive law. The encyclopedia is maintained and updated by an editorial staff. Am Jur has traditionally excelled at covering federal law issues, although it certainly covers state law as well.

1. Researching with Print

As with many complex encyclopedias, Am Jur is best approached using the annually published, multi-volume index. The index will refer you to the location in the encyclopedia where your issue will be discussed. Each volume of the encyclopedia is updated with annual pocket parts.

2. Researching with Westlaw and Lexis

Am Jur is available on WestlawNext by simply entering "am jur" in the universal search bar. Although keyword searching the encyclopedia's full text often retrieves too many irrelevant passages, a nifty feature of the database is the ability to browse the entire table of contents. You may browse the titles and use them as a menu by continuing to select relevant topic and subtopic headings until you reach the encyclopedia text. The most recent updates are available on Westlaw, perhaps within the last few months.

Am Jur is also available as a database on Lexis Advance in the "secondary legal" library. Because Am Jur is currently being published by West, Am Jur on Westlaw may have the most current updates. However, Am Jur on Lexis should be at least as current as the latest pocket part for the print encyclopedia.

C. *Corpus Juris Secundum*

Corpus Juris Secundum (CJS) is another broad, legal encyclopedia attempting to comprehensively state American law by covering all state and federal legal topics. One distinction of CJS is the availability of "black letter" summaries of general rules of law throughout the text. CJS has traditionally been noted for its coverage of state law and exhaustive citations to cases.

1. Researching with Print

As with Am Jur, the annually published, multi-volume index for CJS is the best place to start as you find your way into the text of the encyclopedia. Each volume is updated with an annual pocket part.

2. Researching with Westlaw

CJS is available as a database on WestlawNext by simply entering "CJS" in the universal search bar. The table of contents feature is available for CJS as well as the ability to search the full text with keywords or natural language. CJS is not available on Lexis.

III. Treatises, Practice Guides, and Other Books

Treatises include a wide variety of books about specific areas of law. They may be broadly focused, providing an excellent overview of a topic, or narrowly focused for in-depth analysis. A legal treatise exists for nearly every imaginable legal subject. The value of the information depends upon the reputation and knowledge of the author.

A. *Nutshells*

One of the most basic series of treatises is a publication by West publishing called the "*Nutshell*" series. There are hundreds of *Nutshells*, such as *Contracts in a Nutshell* and *Criminal Law in a Nutshell*. They typically do not provide citations to primary law but rather provide a broad overview of a legal topic, giving a researcher the main ideas and how they may be understood in the broadest context. *Nutshells* are usually authored by law professors, respected for their knowledge in a particular legal subject. An example is *Criminal Law in a Nutshell*, now in its fifth edition, authored by University of North Carolina Law Professor Emeritus, Arnold Loewy. *Nutshells* are national in scope and would rarely if ever provide state-specific information about North Carolina.

B. Hornbooks

Hornbooks, another category of treatises, are typically more detailed in description and explanation of an area of law than a *Nutshell*, although still contained in one volume. They are also usually national in scope and tend to provide the enduring principles of the law in some detail, including limited citations to important statutes or seminal cases from a few jurisdictions in the United States. Sometimes hornbooks are authored by law professors who have also authored a *Nutshell* on the same topic. Examples include *Hazen's Hornbook on the Law of Securities Regulation* and *Calamari and Perillo's Hornbook on Contracts*, both now in a sixth edition, and *Dobbs Hornbook on the Law of Torts*, formerly by Prosser and Keaton. LexisNexis's *Understanding* series and Carolina Academic Press's *Mastering* series both provide a broad overview of a legal subject with limited citations to legal authority and, therefore, serve a similar purpose to hornbooks.

C. Professional Treatises

Professional treatises or "practitioner treatise series" are much more detailed, typically published in multi-volume sets and usually extensively footnoted with citations. These treatises often provide comprehensive description of legal areas in fine detail. Because they often delve beyond the enduring principles and also describe the more rapidly developing areas, they may be updated more often. A number of the authors of hornbooks also publish a more detailed professional treatise version. Other examples of this category include *McCormick on Evidence*, *Nimmer on Copyright*, *Chisum on Patents*, and *Scott on Trusts*.

D. North Carolina Treatises

A number of treatises focus on North Carolina law. These materials are extremely valuable and highly recommended because they are written by legal experts, describe the law in North Carolina, and cite North Carolina primary law such as cases, statutes, or regulations. See Table 3-3 for a list of several examples of North Carolina treatises. There are many others not included in this sampling.[1]

---

1. For a more comprehensive list of North Carolina treatises, see Scott Childs & Nick Sexton, *North Carolina Legal Research Guide* (2d ed., Hein Publ'g 2009).

Table 3-3. Examples of North Carolina Treatises

Brandis and Broun on North Carolina Evidence, 7th ed.

Lee's North Carolina Family Law, 5th ed.

North Carolina Law of Torts, 3d ed. by Daye & Morris

North Carolina Torts, 2d ed. by Logan & Logan

Robinson on North Carolina Corporation Law, 7th ed.

Webster's Real Estate Law in North Carolina, 6th ed.

Wiggins Wills and Administration of Estates in North Carolina, revised 4th ed.

E. Finding Treatises

Although using treatises is relatively easy, finding them may be challenging. A seasoned researcher quickly learns the names of the treatise titles relevant to her field of research; however, when researching an unfamiliar area, locating relevant treatises may be difficult. The easiest approach is to ask someone who regularly researches or practices in the area. For example, in law school, ask a reference librarian or a faculty member. In a law firm, a librarian or an associate who researches in an area would be a good choice. You also might browse a library collection or use an online catalog in a larger library.

Because treatises are based upon the author's hard-earned knowledge and because a great deal of work is involved in the preparation and development of treatises, they are rarely available for free on the Internet. Because of their value, however, some of them are available online for a fee through services such as Westlaw, Lexis, Bloomberg Law, and Loislaw. Browsing the secondary sources area of these online services should lead the researcher to the individual databases, even when the treatise title is unknown.

Once located, either in print or online, treatises are usually best approached using the index or table of contents to find the information needed. Many of the treatises online include a browsable table of contents.

IV. Legal Periodicals

The category of legal periodicals encompasses many different publications. Predominantly, researchers think of legal periodicals as law reviews and journals published by law schools. Almost all of the 203 ABA-approved law schools publish at least one journal and many publish two or more. Law students at these institutions select and edit the articles for publication. Some of the journals publish articles on any subject while others focus on particular legal subjects, such as banking law or the First Amendment.

Typically, the featured articles are written by law professors or knowledgeable practitioners and are heavily footnoted by the authors. The articles may describe the law but more importantly often analyze, compare, and critique the law. The authors sometimes recommend changes in the law. Law student editors also occasionally write articles usually referred to as notes. When articles are focused on a relevant topic in your jurisdiction, the footnoted primary law may provide extremely important research information that can save hours of independent work.

The law schools in North Carolina produce a number of law journals. The schools include the University of North Carolina, Duke University, North Carolina Central University, Wake Forest University, Campbell University, Elon University, and Charlotte School of Law. Some of the journals specifically address North Carolina law and some do not. Some of the journals are subject specific. Law journals from the state's law schools are often excellent secondary sources for relevant legal analysis and critique. Law journals from outside of North Carolina may also publish useful articles as well, such as an article comparing North Carolina law to the law of other states.

A. Free Access on the Internet

Many law school journals have a website where they post the current tables of contents from recent issues. Some journals even post the full text of recent issues. A few journals post substantial collections of journal issues on their webpages. Although this is a free source when available, the quantity and variety of material posted has typically been inconsistent and irregular enough to make it unreliable as a first choice when researching legal journals. Using a journal's website may, however, be a good approach for a researcher seeking a specific, recent article from a specific journal or a researcher who is willing to browse article titles from recent issues of a specific journal.

Another alternative to searching individual sites or using a general search engine such as Google is to use the free, full-text, online law review/journal search engine provided by the Law Practice Division of the American Bar Association[2] This search engine more narrowly focuses on the free, full text of

---

2. www.americanbar.org/groups/departments_offices/legal_technology_resources/resources/free_journal_search.html.

over 400 online law reviews and law journals. Still, the same caveats apply to the comprehensiveness of these searches.

B. Print Indexes

More often, a researcher seeks a relevant law journal article without regard to which journal might have published it and without being limited to only those articles freely posted on the Internet. A wider scope is usually required. Because articles are published in serial fashion and not organized by subject, some type of indexing approach is needed. Traditionally, there have been a number of print indexes of journal articles. The *Index to Legal Periodicals and Books* is an index that began in 1909. Another traditional print index of law journal articles is the *Current Law Index*, which began indexing around 1980. Because print indexes require a lot of expensive shelf space and are cumbersome and time consuming to use, and because there are better alternatives, most law firms and libraries have eliminated print indexes completely in favor of online indexes. If you need to use a print index, seek the assistance of a law librarian.

C. Online Indexes

Among the most common subscription-based online indexes of law journal articles are *LegalTrac*, which provides indexing from over 850 law journals and legal publications since 1980, and an online version of *Index to Legal Periodicals* (ILP), which indexes articles from legal journals, bar publications, and book reviews. ILP is available in several varieties. The standard ILP product includes articles published since 1982. A separate database named *Index to Legal Periodicals Retrospective* covers articles published between 1908 and 1981. A combined product, named *Index to Legal Periodicals & Books: Current & Retrospective*, includes articles published between 1908 and the current period. Many libraries subscribe to either *LegalTrac* or a version of ILP, which are usually available through an online catalog or law firm network.

Westlaw and Lexis both currently provide access to the same legal journal index database, *Legal Resource Index*, which is similar to the print *Current Law Index*. This online journal index does not index any articles prior to 1980. Although the index itself does not contain the full text of articles, if Westlaw or Lexis has the full text of a particular article, the index entry will link to the article within that service. Currently, Bloomberg Law does not include a legal journal index of articles.

D. Full-text Articles on Westlaw and Lexis

Westlaw and Lexis provide large databases of full-text legal journal articles. Bloomberg Law provides access to a significantly smaller database of legal journal articles. More importantly, many students mistakenly search the full-text databases of journal articles on Westlaw, Lexis, or Bloomberg Law, and believe they have searched comprehensively. In fact, there are more articles identified in indexes than there are articles available full text on one of these services. Therefore, searching only the full-text databases on one of these services rather than using an index database is a less comprehensive search. Not only does full-text coverage for many journals not begin until the 1990s, for some years thereafter the coverage may have been only selective rather than comprehensive.

There are differences in searching the indexes and the full-text databases. Each index record includes bibliographic information such as the title, author, date of publication, etc. But the index editors add subject headings—standardized language that may not appear in the title (or text) that might better match your search terms. Alternatively, the full-text databases, while more limited in content, allow you to search every word in every article in each database. However, there are no subject headings or standardized language added to the full-text databases. Which source is better will depend upon your research needs; knowing the differences between these two approaches will facilitate a better decision.

E. HeinOnline

HeinOnline, a relatively new online law journal product, has grown in significance since beginning in 2000. The Hein Publishing Company began scanning full runs of law journals beginning with the first volume of each journal. Within several years, Hein completed this retroactive process. In addition to including the searchable full text of all articles from each volume for each journal, Hein allows you to browse the table of contents for each volume. Most importantly, all the pages are available as PDF images, which many researchers find more comfortable to read online and easier to cite correctly. HeinOnline is a subscription product available at law school libraries and increasingly in law firms.

F. Google Scholar

Google Scholar searches many scholarly databases with Google's powerful search engine, including several databases that include law review articles (such as HeinOnline). It is a free service provided by Google, but it does not include access to the articles unless they are freely available on the Internet. Google Scholar provides links to allow you to purchase the articles and partners with academic libraries to integrate links to materials purchased by the library. Thus, when researchers are on a campus network, Google Scholar will recognize the location of the researcher and provide access through the library's subscription. You can also set up this relationship in the "Library Links" part of Google Scholar settings.

G. Other Types of Legal Periodicals

Most state bar organizations publish a bar journal. The North Carolina State Bar publishes the *North Carolina Bar Journal*. The *Bar Journal* is a quarterly magazine providing a wide array of articles related to law practice and professionalism in North Carolina. There are also bar-related notices such as bar committee actions, ethics opinions, disciplinary actions and rule amendments. The *Bar Journal* is distributed to lawyers licensed to practice in North Carolina. Selected articles may be freely available via a search screen from the North Carolina Bar website, www.ncbar.gov/journal/journal_search.asp. Articles are available from 2002 to the present. The *Bar Journal* is useful to practicing attorneys for current awareness purposes as well as to practitioners and researchers for the valuable articles.

Current awareness is an important issue for practitioners and may occasionally be important to legal researchers. At the national level, several fee-based legal newspapers with associated websites include a combination of free and fee-based information. Examples include the *National Law Journal* (www.nationallawjournal.com) and the *New York Law Journal* (www.newyork lawjournal.com). There are also several free legal news websites, such as *Law.com* (www.law.com) and *FindLaw Legal News* (legalnews.findlaw.com). An example of a North Carolina legal periodical serving a current awareness role is the *North Carolina Lawyers Weekly*, which is a weekly printed newspaper that is also published at a website updated daily at www.nclawyersweekly.com. The website has legal news concerning North Carolina lawyers and cases. It contains a mixture of free and fee-based information. This is an excellent current awareness tool for practitioners and researchers.

H. The Research Process for Periodicals

The basic research process for legal periodicals is the same as for treatises. With luck you might have a citation to a specific article. Westlaw, Lexis, Bloomberg Law, and HeinOnline all allow you to retrieve an article by citation. More often than not, however, you will have to search for articles using keywords. Use an online index such as *Index to Legal Periodicals* or *Legal Resource Index* to locate citations to relevant articles, then either read them online or use the citation to find them in print in a library. As usual, printing is an option from these online services but due to the lengthy nature of most journal articles, printing them on demand can be expensive, environmentally unsound, or both. Consider downloading the articles instead.

If an online index is not available, you can search the full text of articles using keywords. You should check the scope note for the database to learn about the chronological coverage of the database and to learn how the content might otherwise be limited.

V. *American Law Reports*

A. ALR Annotations

American Law Reports (ALR) is a serial publication of selected cases with accompanying annotations focused on a very narrow legal issue. The sixth series is now being published, though annotations from earlier series are still useful research tools. *American Law Reports, Federal* is a separate part of ALR that focuses only on federal law. *ALR International* is another separate series that focuses on issues of world-wide importance, including international law topics.

Although it originally began as a case reporter, ALR is no longer used for that purpose. The value of ALR lies in the *annotations*, essays that are sometimes the length of law review articles. These annotations are narrow in scope, tending to address legal issues of some controversy or issues of law that are interpreted differently across the United States. In addition to describing the law, the annotations also provide links to other recommended secondary sources, such as legal encyclopedias and law journal articles. Because of these references, many researchers find the annotations more useful at the beginning of their research process. Since no effort is made to cover all of American law comprehensively like a legal encyclopedia does, there may not be an annotation directly on point for every legal topic. If an ALR annotation exists for your topic, however, it can be a gold mine of relevant information.

ALR may be used in different ways. ALR annotations are the only source that can provide a list of cases on a specific set of facts with a particular outcome (i.e., which party won). For example, assume you are working on an age discrimination case that turns on the issue of constructive discharge. An ALR can provide a list of cases in which particular facts were held to be a constructive discharge and cases whose facts were held not to be a constructive discharge.[3] Analyzing the cases in this list can help you understand how a particular rule has been applied in your jurisdiction. The annotations usually describe the various interpretations of a point of law throughout the United States, with the different states grouped together by the similar way they've interpreted the relevant law. However, it is possible both in the print version and the online version to isolate the cases from a particular jurisdiction. You can use the index of cases in the annotation organized by state to identify the cases. In this way, ALR can become a state-specific tool.

B. How to Research an Issue in ALR

The process of researching in ALR involves using relevant search terms to examine the index and locate annotations addressing a legal issue. When searching print, use the multi-volume, hardbound index. Annotations from *ALR Federal* are also included in the multi-volume index. For less sophisticated or less obscure issues, you might try the one-volume, paperback ALR Quick Index. A separate one-volume, paperback *ALR Federal* Quick Index is also available.

As in a serial publication like a case reporter, volumes of ALR and *ALR Federal* with new annotations are issued throughout the year. The existing individual ALR volumes are updated with case annotations each year in pocket parts.

Westlaw and Lexis both have ALR databases that include ALR through its sixth series and *ALR Federal* through its second series. The databases are updated weekly with new case annotations. The databases include the multi-volume index as well as Electronic Annotations that are not yet released for

---

3. *Circumstances Which Warrant Finding of Constructive Discharge in Cases under Age Discrimination in Employment Act (29 U.S.C.A. §621 et seq.)*, 93 A.L.R. Fed. 10 (1989).

print publication. Bloomberg Law does not provide access to ALR or *ALR Federal*.

VI. Restatements and Principles— American Law Institute

Restatements are summaries of traditionally common law areas such as contracts, torts, and property. Restatements were initiated because no unifying, broadly applicable statements of law for these subjects existed. Many cases had to be read together in a time-consuming manner to understand the applicable law. *Principles*, introduced in the 1990s, are summaries of areas of law as the drafters would like the law to be. Restatements and Principles are produced by the American Law Institute.

A. The Creation of Restatements and Principles

Restatements and Principles are crafted by a group or committee of scholars, judges and practitioners, usually led by the scholar known as the *reporter*. The reporter organizes the work of the committee in producing a document that states the law. The painstaking process of creating the drafts leading up to a Restatement and the respect earned by the reporter and members of the committee all contribute to the high regard in which Restatements are held. Among secondary sources, Restatements are the most authoritative.

Restatements and Principles are published by subject. See Table 3-4 for a list of the Restatement subjects and Table 3-5 for a list of the Principles subjects. Within each Restatement subject are series, some of which first began in the 1920s. Currently, third series Restatements are being published. Subjects have been added since the first series subjects in the 1920s. It is possible that a subject may be drafted and published for the first time as a second series or a third series, when no previous editions for that subject exist in earlier series.

Table 3-4. Restatement Subjects

Agency

Conflict of Laws

Contracts

Employment Law

Foreign Relations Law of the United States

International Commercial Arbitration

Judgments

The Law Governing Lawyers

Property

Restitution and Unjust Enrichment

Security

Suretyship and Guaranty

Torts

Trusts

Unfair Competition

Table 3-5. Principles Subjects

Aggregate Litigation

Corporate Governance

Election Law: Resolution of Election Disputes

Family Dissolution: Analysis and Recommendations

Intellectual Property: Principles Governing Jurisdiction, Choice of Law, and Judgments in Transnational Disputes

Liability Insurance

Nonprofit Organizations

Software Contracts

B. Researching an Issue in the Restatements or Principles

To begin researching using paper Restatements or Principles, start with the legal subject name. Select the multi-volume set for that subject and look for the index in the last volume before the appendix. Although the text may only be updated every few decades, the cases that cite the Restatements or Principles are updated at least once a year and presented in pocket parts in the back of the books.

Although the Restatements and Principles are not available freely on the Internet, they may be found online on Westlaw and Lexis. For example on West-lawNext, begin typing "restatement" in the universal search bar and a list of the Restatement-related databases will appear. Many of the Restatement subjects are also available as individual databases. Bloomberg Law does not currently provide access to the Restatements or Principles.

To confirm the latest publications in each series, see the American Law Institute website (www.ali.org), which includes a constantly updated publications list. The website also has information about new subjects being added to the latest series of subjects and the various drafts of those new subjects that might be available.

Because the text of the Restatements and Principles is so slowly updated, they are not the best source of information for new or cutting-edge legal issues. However, their value lies in the certainty of the basic information comprising these topics.

VII. Continuing Legal Education Publications

Many states require that each attorney licensed to practice within that state participate in a certain number of hours of classes each year where new or updated information is provided about a particular area of the law. These classes are usually referred to as *continuing legal education* (CLE). Presenters and teachers at these classes often publish their course materials or make them available to attorneys or the public. CLE materials are typically very practical in nature. They either discuss how the law has recently changed or how a legal process or procedure might be better accomplished or improved. The materials have current awareness value and may also be useful for a researcher not familiar with the issues related to a legal subject.

The CLE-sponsoring organization — such as the state bar association, a state law school, or a special organization created to oversee or provide CLE courses — is usually responsible for publishing the information. For example, in North Carolina, the Continuing Legal Education Office of the North Carolina Bar coordinates courses for attorneys and provides publications. The University of North Carolina School of Law produces an annual CLE event with scores of topics covered. The materials from each session are published. In the past, Wake Forest School of Law has also published CLE materials. Many of these materials can be found at the academic law libraries in North Carolina.

Several companies coordinate CLE events at the national level and publish course handbooks. For example, the Practising Law Institute (PLI) sells hundreds of publications from CLE programs via its website (www.pli.edu) and MP3 files are also available. Bloomberg Law provides many of the PLI publications or other CLE-type materials accessible in various databases. Westlaw and Lexis provide other types of CLE materials.

Again, as with many secondary sources, CLE materials are typically not freely available on the Internet.

VIII. Legal Forms

Legal work must often be done in a precise manner. Legal processes that have proved successful over time or been tested in the courtroom are replicated as forms that are acceptable or safe methods of accomplishing certain legal tasks. Several examples of types of documents in which forms are useful include last wills and testaments and certain types of judicial pleadings. By using forms, lawyers or researchers do not have to reinvent the wheel and can be comforted knowing that a particular form has been successful in the past.

The challenge of using forms is to know that you have selected the most applicable form. There are secondary source publications that either include forms or are composed entirely of forms. Some of these form sets also include citations to primary law as authority for use of each particular form. A number of form books are available in academic law libraries. Some forms are also available online, providing the ability to complete the forms online or cut and paste at least portions of them into word processing software.

Most jurisdictions have forms that are specific to the laws and methods of that jurisdiction. While some state-specific collections of forms may not contain the volume or depth of various types of forms found in one of the national form books, the forms available in a state-specific set are more relevant to the unique aspects of that jurisdiction. In North Carolina, the classic form book is *Douglas' Forms*, a five-volume set of three-ring binders with forms addressing a wide range of legal issues. The print set is best approached by using the index at the end of the last volume. *Douglas' Forms* is also available as a set of databases on Lexis. A number of North Carolina treatises include a set of forms specific to that area of North Carolina law. The North Carolina Administrative Office of Courts also provides hundreds of civil and criminal procedure forms at the court website (www.nccourts.org/Forms/FormSearch.asp).

West Legal Forms and *American Jurisprudence Legal Forms, 2d* are examples of national form books. Although not focused on a particular jurisdiction, these form books are very detailed and provide a form that could be adapted to nearly any situation; however, you carry the burden of knowing and understanding exactly what is required in your jurisdiction and meeting your client's needs. These publications and other national form books are available online from Westlaw and Lexis.

A number of companies provide legal forms via the Internet, such as U.S. Legal Forms (www.uslegalforms.com) and FindLaw Forms (http://forms.lp.findlaw.com). Forms of this nature typically are not free but are provided for a small fee, usually less than the cost of having the correct form or document prepared by a licensed attorney. These forms tend to be general in nature but might profess to be appropriate for various jurisdictions. Westlaw, Lexis, and Bloomberg Law all have large collections of forms and sample documents online. These forms are searchable and browsable by topic and jurisdiction. Bloomberg's Dealmaker database is a collection of the best sample documents selected by Bloomberg staff.

Forms might be used extensively in some aspects of law practice, such as pleadings, real estate transactions, and wills and estates. Briefs and memoranda can also serve as forms. Some law firms or organizations maintain brief banks allowing associated members to review a previous researcher's work on a similar legal topic and simply update the work that was done on the original brief or memorandum. This would also be a type of form used in research.

IX. Jury Instructions

Most jurisdictions have prepared standard jury instructions to be used by the judge to instruct the jury in various areas of law relevant to an issue in the trial. The instructions may vary in meaning and interpretation of the law as it applies in different circumstances. When conducting a jury trial, the judge will typically ask the lawyers before or during a trial for their suggested jury instructions. Researchers preparing for a jury trial will often research the standard jury instructions and select the ones most relevant or favorable to their client's case.

The University of North Carolina School of Government began publishing the *North Carolina Pattern Jury Instructions* in the 1960s. The jury instructions are now compiled and updated by the Committee on Pattern Jury Instructions of the North Carolina Conference of Superior Court Judges along with the School of Government. The instructions are updated every year. See Table 3-6 for a list of the categories of instructions.

Table 3-6. *North Carolina Pattern Jury Instructions*

North Carolina Pattern Jury Instructions: Civil

North Carolina Pattern Jury Instructions: Criminal

North Carolina Pattern Jury Instructions: Motor Vehicle

Although the *North Carolina Pattern Jury Instructions* are not available for free on the Internet or in databases on Westlaw, Lexis, or Bloomberg, they are available by subscription from the University of North Carolina School of Government in three-ring binders. The jury instructions are available online through Fastcase and Casemaker. Fastcase is available to North Carolina Bar Association Members at no additional cost. Finally, the instructions are also available digitally from the CX Corporation as a free standing desktop application (www.cx2000.com/Products/tabid/54/Default.aspx). Be sure to check for the latest updates, which are distributed annually.

Federal model jury instructions are available in many libraries and are designed to explain relevant issues of federal law to a jury trying a federal case.

X. Uniform Laws and Model Codes

The National Conference of Commissioners on Uniform State Laws (www.nccusl.org), now known as the Uniform Law Commission (uniform laws.org), is an organization that drafts and publishes uniform laws and model codes for the purpose of harmonizing the law across all fifty states. Each state is responsible for selecting the judges, jurists, professors, or legislators to be members of the Commission. The commissioners attend the national meetings of the Commission to work on preparing and adopting the uniform laws and codes.

The most important example of the Commission's work is the Uniform Commercial Code, which has been widely adopted by states across the country. In addition to the proposed statutory language of each code, the Commission also publishes explanatory notes, drafts, and comments about the proposed code.

Uniform laws and model codes are especially useful if your jurisdiction has adopted one. While each jurisdiction is free to make whatever changes it feels appropriate when adopting the proposed code, the Commission's explanatory notes are often helpful when later attempting to interpret or better understand the provisions at issue.

The most widely available print publication of the Commission's work is a West publication called *Uniform Laws Annotated,* which is also available on Westlaw. The print version is updated at least annually.

XI. Law-related Blogs

A wide variety of legal commentary is available in blogs. Law-related blogs, sometimes called "blawgs," are usually as valuable as the reputations of the authors. Blog commentary from a recognized expert in a legal area could assist a research project in the same way that commentary from a treatise might be used. Even commentary from less well known blog authors could provide useful information when researching a topic. But because blogs are often not edited, you must filter through a great deal of commentary and make your own assessment of the value and quality of the information. This is a common problem when using free resources found using the internet. Additionally, one of the dangers in searching law-related blogs for legal research purposes, besides the challenge of determining the value and quality of the information, is the possibility of using too much time to find information of little relevance.

Potential blog authors or topics can be identified using a search engine such as Google; however, perhaps the best approach to finding quality law-related blogs is to use the Blawg Directory at the American Bar Association Journal website, www.abajournal.com/blawgs. Currently, the directory is browsable by topic, author type, region, and law school. The directory is continuously updated.

Chapter 4

Researching Constitutions

Constitutions are often referred to as "organic documents" because they both authorize and define the government of a particular jurisdiction. In the United States, there is an evolving relationship between the federal government and the governments of the states, generally referred to as "federalism." While the U.S. Constitution is the supreme law of the land, it is limited in scope. The Tenth Amendment of the Constitution defines the relationship between the United States government and the governments of the 50 states in this way: "The powers not delegated to the United States by the Constitution, nor prohibited by it to the States, are reserved to the States respectively, or to the people." The balance of power between the federal government and the states continues to be an important evolving legal issue.

The United States Constitution was adopted by Congress in 1787. A North Carolina state convention in 1788 failed to ratify the U.S. Constitution due to concerns over the lack of a bill of rights and several other issues.[1] North Carolina did not ratify the U.S. Constitution until 1789, becoming the twelfth state to ratify.[2] The new federal government commenced earlier in 1789 under the new U.S. Constitution.

As for the state itself, North Carolina assertively declared its independence from Great Britain in May 1775 when the Mecklenburg County Committee of Safety adopted the "Mecklenburg Resolves."[3] A document allegedly adopted

---

1. *Proceedings and Debates of the Convention of North-Carolina, Convened at Hillsborough, on Monday the 21st Day of July, 1788, for the Purpose of Deliberating and Determining on the Constitution Recommended by the General Convention at Philadelphia, the 17th Day of September, 1787: To Which is Prefixed the Said Constitution* (Hodges and Willis, 1789) available at http://docsouth.unc.edu/nc/conv1788/conv1788.html.

2. Ratification of the Constitution by the State of North Carolina; November 21, 1789. *See* http://avalon.law.yale.edu/18th_century/ratnc.asp.

3. The text of the Mecklenburg Resolves is available at https://archive.org/details/truthjusticeforh00week.

earlier in May of 1775, known as the "Mecklenburg Declaration of Independence" declared the state's independence from Great Britain. However, there is disputed confirmation of this Declaration.[4] The first North Carolina Constitution was adopted in December, 1776.[5]

North Carolina has had three constitutions during its statehood. The first was drafted and adopted by the fifth provincial congress in December, 1776. Significant amendments to the 1776 Constitution were made in 1835. Another constitutional convention in 1862–63 added amendments including secession from the Union. This second North Carolina Constitution was adopted in 1868. The third and current North Carolina Constitution was adopted in 1971. See Table 4-1 for a list of the articles of the current North Carolina Constitution.

Table 4-1. Articles of the North Carolina Constitution

Article I.	Declaration of Rights
Article II.	Legislative
Article III.	Executive
Article IV.	Judicial
Article V.	Finance
Article VI.	Suffrage and Eligibility to Office
Article VII.	Local Government
Article VIII.	Corporations
Article IX.	Education
Article X.	Homesteads and Exemptions
Article XI.	Punishments, Corrections, and Charities
Article XII.	Military Forces
Article XIII.	Conventions; Constitutional Amendment and Revision
Article XIV.	Miscellaneous

---

4. *See* George W. Graham, *The Mecklenburg Declaration of Independence May 20, 1775* (Neal Pub., 1905). The University of North Carolina Wilson Library contains a collection of papers, primarily between 1775 and 1853, "accumulated by Joseph McKnitt Alexander and others relating to the Mecklenburg Declaration and Resolves of May 1775, and the controversy over them, including later testimony of witnesses and copies of documents, papers of North Carolina officials concerning the publication of a pamphlet on the subject in 1831, and later letters related to aspects of the controversy." *See* www.lib.unc.edu/mss/inv/m/Mecklenburg_Declaration.html.

5. Francis Newton Thorp, *The Federal and State Constitutions, Colonial Charters and Other Organic Laws of the States, Territories and Colonies Now or Heretofore Forming the United States of America*, (Government Printing Office, 1909).

I. Researching the 1971 North Carolina Constitution

The easiest and most reliable print sources for the current North Carolina Constitution (1971) are the two annotated statutory codes, *General Statutes of North Carolina Annotated* and *West's North Carolina General Statutes Annotated*. In addition to the current text of the Constitution, both of these sources provide important research annotations such as summaries of and citations to court decisions that have discussed and interpreted the Constitution. The annotations also include a history note, related opinions of the Attorney General, and available citations to related law review or journal articles. Both codes include the North Carolina Constitution at the end of the multi-volume set in a separate volume. Both publications' general indexes also index individual sections of the North Carolina Constitution, which also makes either code a good research tool for the Constitution. The LexisNexis-published *General Statutes of North Carolina Annotated* also includes a "Table of Comparable Sections" relating comparable sections of the 1868 Constitution to sections of the 1971 Constitution.

The North Carolina Constitution is also available online. The two publishers of the North Carolina General Statutes, LexisNexis and West, also provide the same information online at their websites, Lexis Advance and WestlawNext. Bloomberg Law includes the text of the current North Carolina constitution in its North Carolina Legislative database, but that database does not have annotations similar to the LexisNexis or West versions. The current constitution is also freely available from the North Carolina General Assembly website.[6] Although free, this version of the North Carolina Constitution lacks the annotations found in the versions published by LexisNexis and West.

An excellent essay about North Carolina's interesting constitutional history was written by Professor John Orth. This essay is posted on the State Library of North Carolina website and links to an unannotated version of the North Carolina Constitution.[7]

---

6. The constitution is available in PDF at www.ncga.state.nc.us/Legislation/constitution/ncconstitution.pdf.

7. This may be found at http://ncpedia.org/government/nc-constitution-history. *See also* John Sanders, "A Brief History of the Constitutions of North Carolina" in *North Carolina Government, 1585–1979: A Narrative and Statistical History* (John L. Cheney, ed. 1981).

II. Interpreting the North Carolina Constitution

The best starting point for interpreting the North Carolina Constitution is *The North Carolina State Constitution*.[8] This guide provides both a section-by-section analysis of the current North Carolina Constitution and an overview of the process of the writing and ratification of all three North Carolina constitutions.

To the extent that the previous North Carolina constitutions would be useful to understand or interpret the 1971 Constitution, they are available from several sources. The Constitution of 1776 is available in the 1909 classic publication, *The Federal and State Constitutions, Colonial Charters and Other Organic Laws of the States, Territories and Colonies Now or Heretofore Forming the United States of America*, compiled and edited by Francis Newton Thorpe.[9] For a greater treatment of North Carolina colonial documents and sources of the 1776 Constitution, see Chapter 35, "North Carolina Legal Colonial Legal Materials," in *Pre-Statehood Legal Materials, A Fifty State Research Guide*.[10] The 1776 Constitution is also conveniently available online at the Avalon Project, Lillian Goldman Law Library, Yale Law School.[11]

The Constitution of 1868 is available online through the North Carolina Legislative Library.[12]

III. Researching the United States Constitution

As with the North Carolina Constitution, the United States Constitution is best approached using annotated statutes. The official *United States Code* in-

---

8. John V. Orth & Paul Martin Newby, *The North Carolina State Constitution* (2d ed. 2013). This book is part of the Oxford Commentaries on the State Constitutions of the United States. *See also* John V. Orth, *The Law of the Land: The North Carolina Constitution and State Constitutional Law*, 70 N.C. L. Rev. 1759 (1992).

9. Government Printing Office, 1909, under Act of Congress June 30, 1906.

10. This resource is edited by Michael Chiorazzi and Marguerite Most and published by Haworth Press, 2006.

11. The 1776 Constitution can be found online at http://avalon.law.yale. edu/ 18th_century/nc07.asp.

12. The link to this and other North Carolina constitutions is http://www.ncleg.net/ library/Research/nc%20research/constitution.html.

cludes the United States Constitution. The two annotated federal codes, *United States Code Annotated* and *United States Code Service*, provide the Constitution as well as excellent additional annotated information for researchers. These annotations include citations to relevant cases interpreting constitutional provisions and references to secondary sources. For researchers looking for a free resource, an annotated constitution is available from the Library of Congress on the Federal Digital System platform (http://www.gpo.gov/fdsys/). The Library of Congress version is updated every two years.

In North Carolina, both the *General Statutes of North Carolina Annotated* and *West's North Carolina General Statutes Annotated* include a copy of the United States Constitution in both their print and online versions. There are some differences, however. The U.S. Constitution published in the LexisNexis *General Statutes of North Carolina Annotated* is not annotated. In the *West's North Carolina General Statutes Annotated*, the U.S. Constitution has no judicial decision annotations but does have annotations including limited historical notes, cross-references, and "Library References" to related ALR annotations, encyclopedia articles, and West Topic and Key Numbers.

IV. Interpreting the United States Constitution

Many a law professor has made a career out of interpreting the United States Constitution, and multi-volume treatises have been written about it. Seeking one of these treatises would be a good starting point for researching provisions of the U.S. Constitution. Examples of important constitutional law treatises include Nowak and Rotunda's *Treatise on Constitutional Law: Substance and Procedure*, 4th edition, and Lawrence Tribe's *American Constitutional Law*. Although less desirable for efficient research, another obvious approach to interpreting the U.S. Constitution is to find relevant cases interpreting it. Start by finding the relevant section of the U.S. Constitution in one of the two annotated United States Code publications where cases citing and interpreting the Constitution would be listed. The cases will provide direct analysis on specific issues.

Chapter 5

Researching Statutes

Legislators are empowered by the people to operate the legislative branch of government. These elected officials, both representatives and senators in a bicameral legislature like the North Carolina General Assembly, gather together to discuss and debate possible laws that address existing problems, prevent future problems, or improve constituents' lives generally. Legislators attempt to reach consensus by debating, compromising, voting, and enacting laws. Although a few bills are enacted that apply to very few people, enacted law is typically broadly conceived and generally applicable to everyone. Broadly applicable law enacted by a legislature is called *statutory law*. This chapter will address researching statutory law. Chapter 6 will discuss researching documents produced in the legislative process during the creation of statutory law, called *legislative history*.

I. Forms of North Carolina Statutory Law

A bill becomes enacted in North Carolina in one of two ways. A few types of bills may become statutory law after being ratified by both chambers of the North Carolina General Assembly. Ratification involves both chambers passing the identical legislation after it has already been approved separately in both chambers. For most bills, however, the Governor must sign the ratified legislation before it becomes law. The result of either of these processes is that the legislation becomes a session law.

Session laws are published in the sequence in which they are passed in each session of the General Assembly, hence the name session laws. Shortly after they are passed, session laws are integrated into a statutory code that is organized by subject and periodically updated with any changes to the existing statutory law. Without the codification, searching for all the relevant law collected together in one place and currently updated would be extremely difficult. Because of the value provided by codes, most statutory law research is accomplished using codes. However, there are situations in which a researcher might need session laws as well.

A. Session Laws

A *session law* is a bill that has been ratified by the General Assembly, and in most cases, signed by the Governor. Session laws are not annotated but simply contain the text of the law. There are several sources of session laws in North Carolina.

The annual print publication *Session Laws of North Carolina* is available at many state and academic law libraries in North Carolina. The State Library provides access to session laws back to 1817 at http://ncgovdocs.org/guides/ sessionlawslist.htm. Also, many academic law libraries across the country provide access to all fifty states' session laws either through an online service such as HeinOnline or in microfiche. North Carolina session laws are available on HeinOnline from 1715 forward (including the North Carolina Colony laws).

The General Assembly website (www.ncleg.net) is an excellent free source of session laws with a convenient shortcut link on the front page. Session laws can be found at that site dating back to the 1985–86 General Assembly session.

Current North Carolina session laws may be found in both print and online versions of the state code, North Carolina General Statutes, to be discussed in the next section. While the print codes include current session laws in paper pamphlets throughout the year, the codes on Westlaw and Lexis may more quickly integrate the session laws into the statutory codification.

B. Codes

The collection of all the relevant statutory law on a subject together in one location, constantly updated, is a critical tool in the legal research process. These tools are called *codes*. In North Carolina, each section of the statutory code is annotated by the publisher with citations to relevant cases and summaries of those cases interpreting or implementing that code section. The annotations also typically include citations to relevant secondary sources such as law review articles, legal encyclopedias, and *American Law Reports* annotations. If you cannot start a research process with secondary sources and must start with a primary law source, an annotated statutory code would be the next best choice as a starting point.

The statutory code in North Carolina is composed of chapters numbered up to 168. Each chapter is subdivided into subchapters, articles, and sections.

For citation purposes, only the chapters and sections are used. For example, N.C. Gen. Stat. §42-45 refers to chapter 42, section 45 of the code. There are two print editions of the North Carolina statutes, both of which are annotated. LexisNexis publishes the official *General Statutes of North Carolina Annotated*. The other publication of North Carolina statutory law is *West's North Carolina General Statutes Annotated*.

1. *General Statutes of North Carolina Annotated*

The official code for North Carolina statutory law is LexisNexis's *General Statutes of North Carolina Annotated*. This version is published in 23 softbound volumes, which are replaced every two years. The annotations in the code include decisions from the North Carolina Supreme Court and the North Carolina Court of Appeals, and all federal cases arising in North Carolina; state law reviews; *American Law Reports* annotations; and North Carolina Attorney General Opinions. The set also includes a separate, fully annotated, softbound volume "Rules of North Carolina" containing an exhaustive list of court and practice rules.[1]

The entire set is republished every two years, but is kept updated by supplements. In the intervening year, LexisNexis publishes an interim supplement that includes all of the new updates to statutory law and annotations. Every year, the code is periodically updated with the *General Statutes of North Carolina Advance Annotation Service* (AAS) and *General Statutes of North Carolina Advance Legislative Service* (ALS) pamphlets. The AAS pamphlets are published three times a year, providing annotations to the most current case law and journal articles. The ALS is published as warranted by legislative activity and provides the latest session laws as passed by the General Assembly. Each ALS pamphlet includes several tables to assist researchers, such as a Table of General Statutes Chapters with corresponding bill numbers from the newly passed session laws, and a reverse table of bills and the corresponding chapter numbers. The Table of Sections Added, Amended, or Appealed allows you to look up a specific *General Statutes* section number to determine whether any of the new session laws affect it. Finally, the ALS pamphlet includes a cumulative subject index.

Lexis provides the complete contents of the *General Statutes of North Carolina Annotated* in a searchable database on Lexis Advance. The database is also browsable using a table of contents organized by chapter number. You may use this menu approach to link to relevant text of the code.

---

1. For more information about North Carolina rules, see Chapter 10.

A separate database is available for the *Advance Legislative Service*, which is continuously updated. The database provides new session laws throughout the current legislative session within the last several days and has complete session laws back to 1989. Lexis also provides a combined database with the *General Statutes of North Carolina Annotated* and the ALS.

2. West's North Carolina General Statutes Annotated

In 1999, West began publishing an unofficial but very useful codification of North Carolina General Statutes, *West's North Carolina General Statutes Annotated.* The entire statutory text, numbering system, and arrangement of the statutory law is identical to the official version. The annotations differ somewhat between the two codes. West codes typically have more comprehensive case law annotations called "Notes of Decisions." This code also references the *North Carolina Administrative Code* and different analytical products, such as the West Topic and Key Number system and *Strong's North Carolina Index.*

The West code is published in hardbound volumes and updated with annual pocket parts. The annual pocket parts are supplemented throughout the year with *Interim Update* pamphlets that update both the text of the code as new session laws are passed by the General Assembly and the annotations to the existing code. The new information is conveniently organized into the chapter arrangement of the code.

This code is also updated with the *North Carolina Legislative Service*, which is published several times during the legislative session. In addition to providing the text of recently enacted session laws, the *Service* also includes a cumulative statutes table showing the sections of the code affected by the new session laws, a list of the house and senate bills that became the enacted session laws, and a cumulative subject index.

Westlaw provides the complete contents of the *West's North Carolina General Statutes Annotated* in a searchable database on WestlawNext. Like the Lexis Advance version of the code, WestlawNext also provides the chapters in a table of contents form that permits convenient browsing of the code.

Westlaw includes the *West's North Carolina General Statutes Annotated* index that is browsable alphabetically. The Popular Name Table is also available in a browsable, alphabetical arrangement.

3. North Carolina General Statutes from the General Assembly

The North Carolina General Assembly maintains an excellent website with an enormous amount of information produced by and about the activities of

the General Assembly, including a copy of the General Statutes (www.ncga.
state.nc.us/gascripts/Statutes/Statutes.asp).

The version of the North Carolina General Statutes that is available at the
General Assembly site is free. The statutes are searchable and also browsable
by chapter. Several caveats are warranted. The website warns researchers that
the text of the General Statutes found at the site is not official. Only the LexisNexis print version contains the official text of the code. Second, the code
found at this site is not annotated beyond some basic legislative history citations
to session laws associated with the current text of the statutes. Third, the General Statutes version at this site is updated only once a year, after the General
Assembly session ends. Although General Assembly sessions are considered to
extend over a two-year period, each two-year session is composed of a long
session the first year, usually beginning in January of each odd-numbered year,
and a short session the second year, usually beginning in May of each even-
numbered year. The available code at the General Assembly website is updated
only at the end of each of these annual sessions.[2]

4. North Carolina General Statutes on Bloomberg Law

Bloomberg Law maintains a database of the current North Carolina General
Statutes. It is not annotated like the versions on Lexis or Westlaw. To browse
or search it, simply select State Law from the Search & Browse tab. Then, select
North Carolina from the interactive map. The General Statutes are included
in the N.C. Legislative link.

II. Initial Print Research Strategy

Perhaps surprisingly, the overall research process for print and online versions of the General Statutes of North Carolina (and really any statutory law)
is strikingly similar. The initial strategies for print and online research will be
treated separately in Parts II and III of this chapter. Part IV discusses how the
research process continues once you've identified a relevant statute, regardless
of whether you are searching with print or online format.

A. Using a Citation or Popular Name

If you are fortunate enough to have a statutory citation, simply look up the
code section in a print code. For example, the citation N.C. Gen. Stat. § 42-

---

2. Much additional and valuable legislative history information is available from
the website and will be discussed in Chapter 6.

45 means the statute will be found in chapter 42, section 45. Look for the volume that contains chapter 42. Then, page through the volume until you find section 45.

You may occasionally have the popular name of a session law, such as the Midwifery Practice Act. If so, you can find the act in the Popular Name Table in the index volume of the code. The entry will provide basic information about the act describing where the act is codified.

B. Browsing the Index for Search Terms

Without a statutory citation or the popular name of a session law, the researcher must have relevant search terms to use in searching the code.[3] With search terms in hand, use the latest index volumes to find citations to relevant code sections. A good index should contain all important terms within the code. Additionally, the index should include related relevant terms with "see" or "see also" references for those logical terms with which researchers are likely to approach the index, but that don't actually appear in the text. In that way, the index is a superior method of connecting the researcher's search terms with related subjects in the code. It is important to be patient and flexible when using the index. If your first term does not work, try a synonym or broader term.

C. Browsing the Table of Contents for the Chapters

An alternative approach, if you have some understanding of the subject, is to browse the table of contents of the code. In North Carolina, this means browsing the chapters to select the most relevant chapter. The more information you have about the subject of law being researched and the structure of the code, the more likely this approach will be successful.

III. Initial Online Research Strategy

Strategies for researching your issues in online versions of the code are similar but bear some explanation.

---

3. See Chapter 2 for a discussion of the journalistic approach or the TARPP method of developing search terms.

A. Using a Citation or Popular Name

To begin, if you have a statutory citation, simply enter the citation in the online system to retrieve the section. On Lexis Advance and WestlawNext, you can use the universal search bar to find a statute by citation. If this is unsuccessful, be sure you are using the appropriate format. Generally, the *Bluebook* or ALWD format will work. Bloomberg Law, however, requires a special citation format. To retrieve a section of the North Carolina General Statutes, simply type NCCODE followed by the section number into the Go bar.

To begin searching with the popular name of a session law, such as the Midwifery Practice Act, find the act in the Popular Name alphabetical listing available from the North Carolina General Statutes Annotated database search screen on WestlawNext. Alternatively, the popular name could be searched as a phrase in the General Statutes database in Lexis Advance, WestlawNext, Bloomberg Law, or the General Assembly website.

B. Browsing the Index of the Code Online

WestlawNext allows a researcher to browse the index of *West's North Carolina General Statutes Annotated* online. This approach combines the convenience of online access with the value of a human-mediated index. Rather than retrieving only those results that match your exact search terms from a keyword search using terms and connectors, a search of the index will include terms that are not necessarily in the text of the statutes you are searching, but that are logical terms associated with it. This provides a greater opportunity to find relevant documents. This option is not available on Lexis Advance or the General Assembly's website.

C. Searching the Code by Keyword

As with all full-text keyword searching where you will be searching every word in every document in the database, the best practice is to search the smallest database you believe will have all of the relevant documents. If possible, you might at first narrow your keyword search to the specific chapters of the code you believe will have relevant sections. The danger of this approach is that you might miss relevant sections hidden in unlikely chapters of the code. A thorough research process, such as the process discussed in this book, however, will decrease the chances of missing any relevant law.

After selecting the smallest database, develop a well-designed search. On Lexis Advance, you can use pre-search filters to search just North Carolina as the jurisdiction and statute and codes as the type of source. On WestlawNext, select the North Carolina statutes database and then craft a simple or advanced search. A simple search with WestlawNext is more likely to produce relevant results due to the advanced algorithm behind the search. The search engine at the General Assembly website offers few advanced search features compared to Lexis Advance and WestlawNext. In addition, the lack of annotations in the code at the General Assembly website may negatively affect efficient searching. In the databases on Lexis Advance and WestlawNext, the annotations are searched along with the text of the code. The case summaries and other annotations provide additional words related to your subject beyond the text of the statute to which your search terms will be exposed. This feature may enhance the quality of your retrieved results, though it also may result in a high number of irrelevant results. In those rare instances when searching the text alone (without the annotations) is more efficient, both Bloomberg Law and the General Assembly website are good choices.

D. Browsing Chapters as a Table of Contents

After developing some understanding of the legal subject being researched and the structure of the code, the researcher might successfully browse the code's chapters as a table of contents to locate the relevant statutory law. This feature is available online at Lexis Advance, WestlawNext, Bloomberg Law, and at the General Assembly website.

IV. Continued Research Strategy Regardless of Format

After finding a potentially relevant statute, whether using print statutory codes or researching online, follow the research strategy below. This strategy will help you understand the statute and apply it to the facts.

A. Read Statutory Law

Reading statutory language is not like any other legal reading task. Unlike a judicial decision written by a single judge or with the input of a small number of judges, statutory law is created in a legislative process involving large numbers of people often with different viewpoints. Statutory language may be difficult to interpret for a number of reasons. Perhaps language in a statute is intentionally vague for the purpose of achieving the largest number of supporters and therefore being acceptable to the widest range of viewpoints. Alternatively, perhaps the legislators intended to be as specific as possible, but the language they used is simply open to various interpretations. Reading the statute several times is a common necessity, so you understand its provisions and identify any uncertainty.

Several strategies assist researchers in understanding statutes. Both relate to the concept of context. The first strategy is to look for statutory definitions. Statutory definitions may be different from the everyday definitions of words. Go up the hierarchy from the relevant code section to the subchapter or chapter to look for applicable definitions. Reading any definitions might clarify statutory meaning. A second strategy is to take a few minutes and read the individual statute in the context of the surrounding sections and even the entire subchapter. Consider how your section fits into the larger scheme. The added context of the whole might assist you in understanding the meaning of an individual section. Remember that codes are arranged so that laws on similar subjects are located near each other; use this structure to ensure that you are doing thorough research.

B. Find and Read Cases Interpreting the Statute

No matter how carefully you read and understand the meaning of a statute, you must review any judicial decisions that may have interpreted the statute. If a judge in your jurisdiction has interpreted a code section, that interpretation must be either used or challenged. If a judicial interpretation exists, it cannot be ignored.

Both West and Lexis review cases and select a representative sample to include in the annotated versions of their codes (both in print and online). Both publishers attempt to select cases that represent all of the legal issues and novel factual interpretations. West calls these cases "Notes of Decision" and Lexis calls them "Case Notes." They are found with each code section when available and must be examined before the meaning of the statute is ascertained. On West-lawNext, they are included on a separate tab (do not confuse this with the "citing references" tab, which includes all cases, and other sources, that merely mention the code section). When using the print version, this process also includes examining the pocket part and any supplementary pamphlets issued as part of the code. After reviewing all of the case summaries, locate and read each of the relevant cases summarized in the Notes of Decisions or Case Notes since the summaries are not legal authority, but simply an editor's interpretation.

If you are using an unannotated code (such as the one found on the General Assembly's website or on Bloomberg Law), you will have to find the relevant cases yourself using the methods explained in Chapter 7.

C. Interpret and Apply the Statute to the Facts

The court's primary task in interpreting a statute is to ensure that the legislative purpose or intent is achieved. In the absence of any special definitions in the code, this task may be accomplished by examining the statute and giving the language its plain and ordinary meaning. The primary goal of statutory construction is to effectuate the purpose of the legislature in enacting the statute. The first step in determining a statute's purpose is to examine the statute's plain language. Where the language of a statute is clear and unambiguous, there is no room for judicial construction and the courts must construe the statute using its plain meaning.[4]

If the plain and ordinary meaning of the language of the statute does not lead to a reasonable interpretation, the courts in North Carolina have relied on additional guidance. The meaning of the statute may next be determined by its legislative history and the circumstances around the creation of the law suggesting what problem was intended to be addressed by the legislation.[5] See Chapter 6 for a discussion of researching North Carolina legislative history. Another approach to the interpretation of a vague statute is the application of the rules or maxims of statutory construction.[6]

V. Researching Statutes of Other States

Most state jurisdictions codify their statutory law in a similar manner to the method used in North Carolina. There are several states such as New York

---

4. *Cashwell v. Dep't of State Treasurer, Ret. Sys. Div.*, 675 S.E.2d 73, 76 (N.C. App. 2009) (quoting *State v. Hooper*, 591 S.E.2d 514 (N.C. 2004)); *see also* 27 *N.C. Index 4th* Statutes § 23, 2009.

5. *State ex rel. N.C. Milk Comm'n v. Nat'l Food Stores, Inc.*, 154 S.E.2d 548 (1967). For more discussion, *see* Thomas P. Davis, *Legislative History in North Carolina*, 30 Legal Reference Services Quarterly 85 (2011).

6. An analysis of this approach is beyond the scope of this book. For more discussion, see Norman J. Singer, *Statutes and Statutory Construction* (6th ed. 2000), also known as *Sutherland Statutory Construction*.

and Texas that publish their statutory law in volumes by subject rather than by an overall numbering scheme. But otherwise, the research strategies discussed in this chapter would apply directly in those and other states as well.

Lexis Advance,WestlawNext, and Bloomberg Law provide convenient, if expensive, online access to all fifty states' codes. Also, some academic law libraries still collect print versions of or provide online access to all fifty states' codes. Like North Carolina, many states provide an unofficial, unannotated version of their state's code on the Internet. Most states' free statutory code may be retrieved using Google or another search engine. There are also some "mega" websites with convenient links to free legal information that might organize access to free state statutory codes. Such sites include FindLaw (www.findlaw.com) and Cornell's Legal Information Institute (www.law.cornell.edu).

VI. Researching Federal Statutes

Federal statutes are researched in much the same fashion as state statutes. Laws that are enacted by the United States Congress are known as *public laws*.[7] They are first printed as *slip laws* which are simply individually published acts of Congress. Eventually, slip laws are published at the end of the legislative session in *Statutes at Large*, which serves the same function as the *North Carolina Session Laws* publication. Next, the new statutes are codified and incorporated into the federal statutory code, the United States Code, where they are arranged by subject.

Public laws are freely available almost immediately upon adoption on the Federal Digital System (http://www.gpo.gov/fdsys/), called FDsys, a website maintained by the Government Printing Office. Public laws are also quickly available on the Westlaw and Lexis websites. In the research process, public laws serve as a snapshot of a statute as it was originally passed by Congress. Public laws serve little research purpose because a researcher usually wants the most currently updated version of the statute and needs to see the statute in the context of the other related statutes concerning that subject. Therefore, rather than using *Statutes at Large* or public laws online for general statutory research, you will most often use one of the versions of the United States Code. If, however, you want to find an older version of a law or a type of law that

---

7. Occasionally Congress enacts a Private Law, that is, a law that applies only to persons named in the law. These are published as slip laws and collected in the *Statutes at Large*. Private laws do not appear in the U.S. Code.

does not make it into the code (i.e., federal appropriations or temporary and private acts) *Statutes at Large* is a good place to start.

A. *United States Code*

The *United States Code* (USC) is the official federal statutory code, published by the government, arranged by subject comprising 51 titles. The USC is published every six years. In the intervening years, an annual one-volume supplement is published, which contains all changes to the code. Typically, the supplements are several years out of date by the time they are published. Practitioners cannot rely on information this old. The USC is not annotated with related secondary sources and important case summaries explaining how the statute has been interpreted. Fortunately, several privately published versions of the United States Code are updated more often and have many additional benefits discussed below. Therefore, the official USC has limited usefulness in the research process, as most researchers turn to one of the privately published annotated codes. Many courts, however, still require documents submitted to them to cite the official USC.

The United States Code is online at no charge in several places. Scans of the print USC (including supplements) are available on FDsys. A more up-to-date version is available from the Office of Law Revision Council, the entity that creates the USC (http://uscode.house.gov/browse.xhtml). The USC is also available from the Legal Information Institute (www.law.cornell.edu/uscode). It does not have annotations, but is kept up to date.

B. *United States Code Annotated* and *United States Code Service*

There are two versions of an annotated federal code. West publishes the *United States Code Annotated* (USCA) and LexisNexis publishes the *United States Code Service* (USCS). Although unofficial, the statutory text of the USCA or USCS should be identical to the official *United States Code*. They are both annotated with extensive summaries of cases interpreting the statutes (called Notes of Decision) and citations to those cases. Other annotations include references to relevant regulations and secondary sources such as relevant legal encyclopedia articles and ALR annotations. There are some differences in the two versions, though. The USCA includes references to appropriate Topic and Key Numbers from the West Digest System, which can be important in the research process. Also, the associated Topic and Key Numbers can be used to find relevant cases in all jurisdictions through the West Digest System either in print or on WestlawNext. The USCS includes more references to regulations for each section. Bloomberg Law offers an unannotated, but current, version of the U.S. Code.

C. Print Research Strategies for Federal Statutes

The *United States Code Annotated* (USCA) and the *United States Code Service* (USCS) are both published in large multi-volume sets. They are both updated by annual pocket parts placed in the back of each volume. Both publishers issue quarterly supplementary pamphlets throughout the year providing updated text and case annotations. The updating process, when using either of these unofficial print versions, includes examining the pocket parts as well as any supplementary pamphlets. Fortunately, these privately published versions are updated promptly, especially compared to the official USC.

The following research strategies are applicable to both USCA and USCS unless otherwise noted.

1. Retrieving by Citation or Popular Name

You may approach the annotated statutes with a citation, such as 28 USC § 1331, obtained from some other source. First, scan the books for the volumes containing title 28 and then find the individual volume that contains section 1331.

A second, similar type of retrieval is the use of a public law's popular name. When you know the name of the original legislation that is now codified, such as the Clean Air Act, use the Popular Name Table to find where the act was codified. For this act, there are many amendments that will also be listed under the name of the act in the table. These references will lead you to the current version of the legislation, generally grouped will all the legislation on that subject and currently updated.

2. Searching the Index

Most often you will approach the USC without a citation or popular name. When you only have a subject to work with, use the index to locate your subject in the federal code. The index is finely detailed and updated continuously throughout the year. This option has the value of human intermediation. For example, a statute concerning the prevention of juvenile crime would be indexed under several relevant terms in addition to "juvenile," the term used in the statute. Additional indexed terms associated with this statute might include other common terms for juvenile such as child, youth, adolescent, or teenager.

3. Browsing the Titles

Another approach is to simply select the appropriate title and volume from the shelf and browse the table of contents for that title located in the front of the volume(s). This approach is usually more successful when you have substantial familiarity with the code and an understanding of the area of law being researched. Also, this approach is easier when researching some legal issues than others. For example, when researching a copyright problem, you might know that the copyright statutes are contained in title 17. However, some legal subjects are subsumed in USC titles that belie their name or may be spread across several different titles.

D. Online Research Strategies for Federal Statutes

As a West publication, the *United States Code Annotated* is also found on WestlawNext. The *United States Code Service* is on Lexis Advance. Several search options are available using these online sources. An unannotated, but current, version of the U.S. Code is available on Bloomberg Law.

1. Using a Citation or Popular Name to Search the United States Code

Just as you would enter a citation to retrieve a *North Carolina General Statutes* section, enter a United States Code citation in the online system to retrieve a specific USC section.

The popular name of a public law you are researching can be a gateway into the United States Code. To browse the Popular Name Table on WestlawNext, link to it from the *United States Code Annotated* search and browse screen. Although LexisAdvance does not provide a popular name table for the United States Code at this point, you can type the popular name in the universal search bar to retrieve the Public Law, which includes references to the U.S. Code in Notes throughout the document. There is also no popular name table on Bloomberg Law. You may, however, be able to find the Public Law and a chart detailing where the Public Law is found in the U.S. Code by typing the popular name in the Go bar. If such information is available, it will appear in the Quick Links section of the Go bar.

2. Browsing the Index of the United States Code Online

WestlawNext allows browsing the index of the *United States Code Annotated* online from the USCA search and browse screen, combining the convenience of online access with the value of a human index. The index may include your search terms that appear in documents and terms that are not necessarily in the text of the statutes you are searching, but that are logical terms associated with it. Neither Lexis Advance nor Bloomberg Law provides this index option.

3. Searching the Code by Keyword

Select the smallest set of the United States Code that you believe will have all of the relevant code sections. Develop your search using advanced search options such as phrase searching. Generally, a simple search in WestlawNext will produce relevant results because of the sophisticated algorithm. Lexis Advance produces many results, including relevant ones, with a simple search. A keyword search in Bloomberg Law may miss relevant sections because of the difficulty in conducting a thorough terms and connector search in statutes (especially when you are not familiar with the legal terminology used in the code). This is exacerbated by the lack of an annotated code. If you use Bloomberg Law for statutory research, be sure to compensate by being particular vigilant in your case and secondary source research.

4. Browsing Titles as a Table of Contents

With some understanding of the legal subject being researched and the structure of the United States Code, you might successfully browse the code's titles as a table of contents to locate the relevant statutory law. This feature is available online. This method has the value of seeing the related chapters and sections in context for better understanding of how the relevant code section fits within the statutory law of that legal topic. At any point along this narrowing menu path in WestlawNext and Lexis Advances, you may also engage in keyword searching of that part of the code.

Chapter 6

Researching Legislative History

Chapter 5 discussed researching statutory law. This chapter provides a summary of the process by which statutory law is created in North Carolina. An understanding of the legislative process will assist you in finding the legislative documentation produced in making statutory law as well as interpreting the meaning of that law.

Once you are armed with an understanding of the North Carolina legislative process, the chapter next discusses tracking of current legislation as it proceeds through the legislative process. The steps involved in finding the current details of a bill or the status of a bill in the legislature will be described. This information is useful for researchers with a stake or great interest in current legislation.

A more complex task involves using your understanding of the legislative process to gather a complete legislative history for a particular statute. Legislative history research is particularly important when you are trying to determine the meaning of a vague or ambiguous statute. Researching the legislative history of a statute is among the most difficult state research tasks to accomplish. States typically produce less documentation of the legislative process, and the documentation has traditionally been difficult to access. The state of North Carolina is no exception. Fortunately, the development of online resources has greatly improved access to the documentation produced in the legislative process.

Although there are similarities between the North Carolina legislative process and the legislative process of the United States Congress, the differences are sufficient to warrant separate treatment of the U.S. process at the end of this chapter.

I. Introduction to the North Carolina Legislative Process

Like many states, North Carolina has a bicameral legislature known as the General Assembly. The General Assembly is composed of two chambers, the House of Representatives and the Senate. The House is composed of 120 members elected for two-year terms each even-numbered year. The Senate is composed of 50 members also elected for two-year terms each even-numbered year. Each chamber does much of its work in committees made up of legislators. Each chamber is also supported in its legislative work by a staff of non-legislators who assist with the process.

Each General Assembly meets for a two-year session. The first (or long) session of a General Assembly begins in January of each odd-numbered year and may meet for five or six months. The second (or short) session of a General Assembly convenes each even-numbered year beginning in May and often meets for several months. Later that same year, new statewide elections are held to elect senators and representatives for the next General Assembly. See Table 6-1 for a description of the legislative process and the corresponding documentation.

II. Tracking Current North Carolina Legislation

Researchers commonly need to locate current information about legislation pending in the General Assembly. An attorney may be following a relevant subject related to her practice generally, or perhaps following information relevant to a pending case or client's interest. The process of locating information concerning the status of bills is generically referred to as *bill tracking*. In this process, the researcher typically finds various versions of a bill and learns of the latest activity concerning the bill in the legislative process. There are several sources of bill tracking information.

A. The General Assembly Website

The General Assembly has an excellent website (www.ncleg.net) where an enormous amount of current bill information may easily be found.

1. Tracking by Bill Number

The easiest way to track a bill is to use the bill number. From the General Assembly homepage (www.ncleg.net), select the current session and enter the bill number in the "Find Bills by Number" search box. In addition to the various

Table 6-1. Documenting the North Carolina Legislative Process

Legislative Action	Documentation of the Process
A citizen, interest group, or legislator may promote an idea for a bill.	
The General Assembly leadership may appoint a committee to investigate the idea and submit a study report, identifying the need for the legislation.	**Study reports**, when available, are an important piece of the legislative history of a bill in North Carolina. They provide intent and reasons why legislation should be passed.
The bill may be drafted by any competent person, but there are two separate governmental organizations designated to draft bills. The Office of the Attorney General must draft bills for the state departments and agencies, including the General Assembly. The General Assembly also has a support agency, the Legislative Services Commission, which has a Bill Drafting Division serving the needs of the legislators.	The **bill text**, if the bill is adopted, is the actual body of language of the statute. Different versions of the bill as it passes through the legislative process might shed light on legislative intent.
The bill is introduced in either chamber of the General Assembly by a member of that chamber. The Reading Clerk reads the name of the sponsor, the bill number, and the bill title aloud on the floor of the chamber. This is the first reading.	The bill must be placed on the **House** or **Senate calendar** to be introduced.
The bill is assigned to a committee or subcommittee for deliberations.	
If the committee or subcommittee decides to favorably report the bill out of committee, it is returned to the floor of the chamber where a second and third reading take place, possibly with some deliberation.	There is no explanatory report. Committee hearing transcripts are not made, although hearings are recorded. The committee's secretary creates brief **committee minutes** from the recording and files the minutes with the Legislative Library. The recordings are not retained. The Library supports the Assembly but is open to the public.

That chamber might vote to pass the bill after several more readings. If not, the bill dies. If the chamber passes the bill, it is *engrossed* in that chamber and the bill moves to the second chamber in the General Assembly.	As with hearings, North Carolina does not produce a transcript of floor debate. Instead summaries of daily activities are recorded in the **House Journals** and **Senate Journals**. Final vote tallies are also recorded there. Individual voting records for each bill and legislator for each session are available at the General Assembly website. The "Bill Reports" page at the General Assembly website links to "**House Bills passed in the House**" and "**Senate Bills passed in the Senate**." North Carolina provides live audio debate from either chamber. Senate debate is audio-recorded, and those tapes are transferred to the State Archives at the end of a biennial legislative session. Any recordings of House debate are not retained.
In the second chamber, the bill has its first reading and assignment to committee.	
The second chamber's committee may have a hearing. If the bill is reported out of the committee, it is returned to the floor of the second chamber where a second and third reading take place.	As in the first chamber, there is no explanatory report from the committee. Committee hearing transcripts are not made, although hearings are recorded. The committee's secretary creates brief **committee minutes** from the recording and files the minutes with the Legislative Library. The recordings are not retained.
The second chamber may either vote to pass the bill, pass the bill with amendments, or not pass the bill. Generally, the bill dies if not passed. If the bill is passed with amendments, then the bill is returned to the first chamber, which will either concur in the amendments or reject them.	Because North Carolina does not produce a transcript of floor debate, the best record of floor chamber action is the summaries of daily activities recorded in the **House Journals** and **Senate Journals**. Final vote tallies are also recorded there. Individual voting records for each bill and legislator for each session are available at the General Assembly website The "Bill Reports" page at the General Assembly website also links to "**House Bills passed in the Senate**" and "**Senate Bills passed in the House**."

If the first chamber rejects the amendments from the second chamber, a conference committee is created composed of members of both chambers to resolve the differences. If the differences are not resolved, the bill dies.	
If the second chamber passes the bill, or the bill is passed by the conference committee, then both chambers must pass the final bill. The bill is now *enrolled*.	**Enrolled bills** are available from the General Assembly website by bill number.
The enrolled bill is then signed by the presiding officer of each chamber and becomes a *ratified bill*.	**Ratified bills** are available from the General Assembly website by bill number.
Ratified bills are referred to the Governor for his or her signature. (In North Carolina, however, a small number of ratified bills become law without the Governor's signature.)	A list of "**Ratified Bills Pending on the Governor's desk**" is available at the website.
If the Governor signs the bill, it becomes law. If the Governor fails to act on the bill within 10 days while the General Assembly is in session, the bill becomes law. The Governor may veto the bill.	Bills signed by the Governor are identified as "**Chaptered Bills**" on the General Assembly website. A chart of "**Vetoed Bills**" also available at the site.
If the Governor vetoes the bill, the bill is returned to the original chamber where three-fifths of those members present and voting may override the veto. If so, the bill is sent to the second chamber where three-fifths of those members present and voting may also vote to override the veto. If the override vote is successful, the bill becomes law. If not, the bill dies.	
After the bill becomes law, it is given a chapter number and is published as part of the North Carolina Session Laws for that General Assembly session.	

versions of the bill, the retrieved results include the current status of the bill, the bill's sponsors, the vote history of the bill, and a running record of all the activity that has occurred concerning the bill since it was first introduced. The information is usually updated within a day or two during the legislative session. Bill reports, with bill tracking information, are available for bills beginning with the 1985 General Assembly session. See Figure 6-1 for an example of a bill report for House Bill 9, which went on to become Session Law 2009-135, "No Texting While Driving."

Figure 6-1. Bill Report for House Bill 9/Session Law 2009-135

House Bill 9 / S.L. 2009-135 (= S96)

2009-2010 Session

No Texting While Driving.

Text	Fiscal Note
Filed [HTML]	-
Edition 1 [HTML]	-
Edition 2 [HTML]	-
Edition 3 [HTML]	-
Ratified [HTML]	-
SL2009-135 [HTML]	-

Status:	Ch. SL 2009-135 on 06/19/2009

Sponsors	
Primary:	Pierce; Harrison; Hall;
Co:	K. Alexander; M. Alexander; Allred; Bell; Brown; Bryant; Carney; Cleveland; Dickson; Dollar; Earle; England; Farmer-Butterfield; Fisher; Goforth; Goodwin; Hurley; Jackson; Jones; Justice; Luebke; McLawhorn; Spear; Starnes; Tarleton; Underhill; Weiss;

Attributes:	Public; Text has changed;

Vote History								
Date	Subject	RCS #	Aye	No	N/V	Exc. Abs.	Exc. Vote	Total	Result
04/16/2009 2:39PM	Third Reading	[H] - 177	104	5	5	6	0	109	PASSED
06/09/2009 3:30PM	Second Reading	[S] - 542	30	18	1	1	0	48	PASSED

Viewing Last 2 Vote(s)   *View All Votes*

History		
Date	Chamber	Action
01/29/2009	House	Filed
02/02/2009	House	Passed 1st Reading
02/02/2009	House	Ref To Com On Rules, Calendar, and Operations of the House
02/12/2009	House	Withdrawn From Com
02/12/2009	House	Ref to the Com on Ways & Means / Broadband Connectivity, if favorable, Judiciary III
04/02/2009	House	Reptd Fav Com Substitute
04/02/2009	House	Re-ref Com On Judiciary III
04/14/2009	House	Reptd Fav
04/14/2009	House	Cal Pursuant Rule 36(b)
04/14/2009	House	Placed On Cal For 4/15/2009
04/15/2009	House	Amend Adopted 1
04/15/2009	House	Passed 2nd Reading
04/16/2009	House	Amendment Withdrawn 2
04/16/2009	House	Amend Adopted 3
04/16/2009	House	Passed 3rd Reading
04/20/2009	Senate	Rec From House
04/20/2009	Senate	Ref To Com On Judiciary II
05/19/2009	Senate	Reptd Fav
05/19/2009	Senate	Re-ref Com On Appropriations/Base Budget
06/03/2009	Senate	Withdrawn From Com
06/03/2009	Senate	Placed On Cal For 6/9/2009
06/09/2009	Senate	Passed 2nd & 3rd Reading
06/10/2009		Ratified
06/11/2009		Pres. To Gov. 6/11/2009
06/19/2009		Signed By Gov. 6/19/2009
06/19/2009		Ch. SL 2009-135

2. Other Tracking Options on the Website

Also from a convenient search box at the General Assembly main website, the researcher can perform a simple bill text search by first selecting the session, and then entering relevant keywords expected to be found in the text of the bill or bill title. The result retrieved is a set of bills that will provide the same detailed current status information about bills described above when searching by bill number.

Additionally, by selecting the "Legislation/Bills" link (www.ncleg.net/Legislation/Legislation.html) from the homepage, a researcher may search for bills in various ways, including browsing the current status of bills at the "Bill Reports" page (www.ncleg.net/Legislation/BillReports.html) in the following ways: bills with actions in the current session, House bills passed in the House, House bills passed in the Senate, Senate bills passed in the Senate, Senate bills passed in the House, bills in conference, bills to be ratified, and chaptered bills by bill number. The General Assembly "Bill Reports" page also links to a list of ratified bills currently pending on the Governor's desk as well as a list of bills already signed by the Governor.

B. Other Online Sources for Tracking North Carolina Legislation

Although the freely accessible General Assembly website generally provides the most convenient and current tools for bill tracking, several other sources for bill tracking information exist.

1. WestlawNext

WestlawNext contains a North Carolina bill tracking database, "North Carolina Bill Tracking." This database contains a summary and legislative chronology of individual bills from the current legislative session and is updated daily. Bill tracking information from previous General Assembly sessions is available back to 2005 in a separate database called "North Carolina Bill Tracking: Historical" on WestlawNext. Note that the free North Carolina General Assembly website's coverage extends back to 1985.

2. Lexis Advance

Lexis Advance contains a database known as "North Carolina Bill Tracking Reports." The database contains a summary and legislative chronology of individual bills from the current legislative session. It is updated daily. A search of this database may be combined with a search of current session full-text bills in the database. To find bill status and chronology information on Lexis from previous General Assembly sessions, select the database "North Carolina Legislative Bill History" for coverage back to 2002. Note that the free North Carolina General Assembly website's coverage extends considerably farther back to 1985.

3. Bloomberg Law

Bloomberg Law does not contain North Carolina bills or any source of legislative history at this time.

C. Calling or Visiting the Bill Status Desk

Any interested person may get information on the status of current legislation from the Bill Status (Video) System by contacting the Bill Status Desk in the Legislative Library by telephone at (919) 733-7779 or in person in room 2226 of the State Legislative Building.

D. Other Options for Tracking Current North Carolina Legislation

1. Legislative Week in Review

UNC-TV has recently produced a television show called *Legislative Week in Review* (www.unctv.org/content/legweek). The show includes reporting of issues related to legislative activities of the week and interviews with lawmakers. The show also includes examination of pending legislation and an analysis of the week's events. The website features additional information and streaming video from the show. Video archives of the weekly episodes of UNC-TV's *Legislative Week in Review* are available. Typically, the videos at the website are made available on the Monday following the weekend broadcast of the television show.

2. Legislative Reporting Services from the University of North Carolina School of Government

The University of North Carolina School of Government has established a reputation for excellent reporting on legislative activities for 60 years. One of its premier contributions is the *Daily Bulletin*. The *Daily Bulletin* is emailed to subscribers each evening after a legislative day, summarizing every bill introduced that day with the bill number, sponsor, and General Statutes of North

Carolina chapters affected by the bill. The *Bulletin* also includes every amendment, committee substitute, and conference committee report adopted for each bill in each chamber. All daily action taken on the floor of each chamber is also included.

The school also publishes the *Weekly Status Report*, emailed to subscribers, and *North Carolina Legislation*, a summary of each legislative session published approximately four months after the end of each session.

III. Researching North Carolina Legislative History

A. Why Research Legislative History?

Statutory law is often designed to be generally applicable to a wide variety of circumstances, for example, to prevent a wrong or describe a mandatory way of accomplishing a particular outcome. A relevant statute, once located, must be interpreted and applied in each research situation. Sometimes the language and meaning of the statute is clear. Sometimes, however, the meaning or applicability of the statute may be difficult to interpret. This may be due to the nature of the legislative process, which often requires compromise in the selection of specific words in order to achieve a consensus in the legislature to enact the statute. Another reason why statutory language may be difficult to interpret and apply is that the situation in which the statute is being applied may not have been contemplated by the legislators when they drafted the language of the statute.

The rule on statutory interpretation in North Carolina was best stated by the North Carolina Supreme Court in the 1967 case *State ex rel. North Carolina Milk Commission v. National Food Stores*, and has been cited many times.

> While the cardinal principle of statutory construction is that the words of the statute must be given the meaning which will carry out the intent of the Legislature, that intent must be found from the language of the act, its legislative history and the circumstances surrounding its adoption which throw light upon the evil sought to be remedied.[1]

---

1. 270 N.C. 323, 332, 154 S.E.2d 548, 555 (1967).

B. Methods of Researching Legislative History

1. State Sources

Legislative history research is best done by working backward from the finished product, a statute. This process is outlined in Table 6-2 and explained below.

Table 6-2. Process of Legislative History Research

Step 1	Identify the session law numbers.
Step 2	Read the session law text.
Step 3	Review the bill chronology and earlier versions of the bill from the North Carolina General Assembly website. For pre-1985 bills, create the chronology of events using the *House* and *Senate Journals*.
Step 4	Review committee minutes.
Step 5	Review notes from floor debate or actions in *House* and *Senate Journals*.
Step 6	Read any study reports that are available.
Step 7	Read the Governor's signing statement or reported comments if available.

a. Session Law Number

In North Carolina, both of the state codifications of statutory law (*General Statutes of North Carolina Annotated* and *West's North Carolina General Statutes Annotated*) and even the free General Statutes on the General Assembly website provide references to the session laws that added and amended the current statute at issue. This is labeled as the history in the General Statutes of North Carolina and appears just after the statutory text in all versions. Researchers typically use one of these codes when researching statutes, either online or in print, and can easily identify the relevant session law number(s) that added or amended the statute. When using the statutes on WestlawNext, it is important to note that statutes enacted before 1943 have no note, so you must consult another source to obtain session law information.

b. Session Law Text

Identify the session law numbers at the end of the statute. For example, "(1983, c. 701, s. 1.)" refers to section 1 of chapter 701 of the 1983 *Session*

Laws. Also, "(2005-344, s. 1)" refers to section 1 of chapter 344 of the 2005 *Session Laws.* Using the session law numbers found at the end of the statute being researched in the General Statutes, locate the text of the original session law as passed by the General Assembly, and the text of any session laws making subsequent amendments to the statute. Refer to Chapter 5 for specific instructions on finding North Carolina session laws.

Read the session law text to confirm and identify which particular session law (or portions of a session law) are relevant to the legal issue being researched. Remember that a single code section can be the end result of many session laws. To do thorough legislative history research, you must determine which session laws enacted or changed the particular part of code at issue.

c. Final Bill and Previous Versions

The text of each session law also includes the bill number for the House or Senate bill that eventually became that session law. Using this bill number, go to the North Carolina General Assembly website (www.ncleg.net) and retrieve the bill. There is a convenient "Find Bills by Number" search box on the homepage for each General Assembly session going back to 1985. The associated bill report is simply a chronological history of the bill as it traveled through the legislative process, not an actual statement about the intent behind the legislation. See Figure 6-1 for an example of a bill report from the General Assembly website. The report may contain links to earlier versions of bills. These various versions of the bill that were rejected or amended through the process may shed light on the legislative intent. While there may not be convenient hypertext links to other related documentation (e.g., committee minutes, the names of the committees, and dates of the bill being reported out of committee), the information in the report could be useful in locating these additional documents.

d. Pre-1985 Bill Reports

For pre-1985 bills, such a chronology as described in the bill report above must be created by hand using the *House Journals* and *Senate Journals.* The journals index bills and include the page numbers in the journal containing a summary from each day of the session of any action on the particular bill being researched. The State Library of North Carolina makes the journals available online (http://ncgovdocs.org). Academic law libraries and several of the state government libraries have print copies of the North Carolina *House Journals* and *Senate Journals.* The General Assembly also makes journals from 1985 to present available on its website. On WestlawNext, the "North Carolina Legislative History Journals" database has House and Senate journals back to 2001 but currently no more recent than 2006. Lexis Advance does not provide access to the journals.

e. Committee Minutes

From the bill chronology or report, identify the name(s) of the committee(s) that deliberated about the bill. Brief committee meeting minutes might be available at the Legislative Library in Raleigh. The minutes might also include staff member notes or background reports. Minutes of Standing Committees are available from 1967 to the present.

Minutes of specially appointed non-standing and study committees are available from 1963 to the present. As minutes are microfilmed or otherwise reformatted, these collections shift and the dates of coverage may change. Minutes may be unavailable for periods of time as they are reformatted.[2]

f. Floor Debate

The General Assembly provides links for listening to live floor debate in either the Senate or the House. Access is available from the General Assembly homepage. The House floor debate for the current session is audio recorded and archived on the web, which may be accessed from the House page (www.ncga.state.nc.us/House/House.html). Although the Senate audio records its daily floor debate, the recordings are not currently available archived on the webpage. Rather, the audiotapes are transferred to the State Archives, where they can be accessed at the end of the biennial session.

Although the General Assembly does not provide a verbatim written transcript of floor debate, summaries of floor actions are recorded in the *House* and *Senate Journals*.

g. Study Reports

The General Assembly leadership or the Governor may appoint ad hoc study committees or commissions. Likewise, a standing committee of the General Assembly might also be directed to study an issue. Once information is collected, a study report is issued.[3] A study report might explain the need for specific legislation and give the General Assembly guidance in legislatively

---

2. For more precise information about the contents and availability of these materials, consult the chart posted at http://www.ncleg.net/library/LegHistMaterials/leghistmaterials.html.

3. North Carolina study reports are somewhat akin to United States congressional committee prints at the federal level, although in addition to the factual findings, there may be more recommendations than found in a federal committee print.

addressing an issue. The report will often include findings, recommendations, and perhaps even a proposed bill draft. Therefore, the report might provide some context for understanding the intent of the General Assembly behind related legislation.

Many of the recent study reports are available online, just not in one place. Selected, recent study reports are available online at the General Assembly website (www.ncleg.net), accessible from the "Legislative Publications" link. Coverage begins with selected study reports made to the 2001 General Assembly. University of North Carolina has digitized selected study reports. They are available only through the University's Library catalog (http://search.lib.unc.edu/). Adding the phrases "North Carolina General Assembly" and "Legislative Research Commission" to the search will ensure that you receive only study reports in your results.

Print copies of study reports can be identified by viewing an online list of report titles from the Legislative Library (www.ncleg.net/library/Collections/studies/year.html) beginning more comprehensively with reports issued in 1967, with some scattered reports prior to that date. The list of titles is arranged both by year and by subject. The print study reports are available for viewing at the Legislative Library in Raleigh. A select few other libraries may have a smaller collection of the reports, predominantly the North Carolina Supreme Court Library, also in Raleigh.

Several agencies of the General Assembly, such as the Legislative Research Commission and the General Statutes Commission, also may make recommendations for specific legislation. A collection of reports or minutes from these commissions may also be found at the Legislative Library.

h. Governor's Statements

Gubernatorial statements concerning North Carolina legislation are not very common and difficult to locate.[4] The Governor's website provides access to written press releases and audio/video releases that might on occasion relate to legislation. The Governor's public statements about legislation might also be recorded by local media, such as the Raleigh *News and Observer* newspaper (www.newsobserver.com).

Eventually, a North Carolina Governor's public papers and statements will be published by the North Carolina Department of Cultural Resources; however, there is a significant delay in the publication of these materials and they are not widely available.

---

4. In contrast, presidential signing statements are readily available at the federal level.

The Governor was not granted veto power until 1997. Vetoes and veto messages transmitted to the General Assembly are noted in the bill tracking report on the General Assembly's website and include a link to the full text of written statements. A chart of North Carolina's veto history and statistics may be found at http://www.ncleg.net/library/Documents/VetoStats.pdf.

2. WestlawNext and Lexis Advance as Sources of Legislative History

WestlawNext and Lexis Advance provide less precise options for researching North Carolina legislative history. WestlawNext provides a database, "North Carolina Legislative History," which includes different types of information such as bill summaries, *House Journals, Senate Journals,* House vote transcripts, and Governor's statements (such as veto messages and press releases generally beginning between 2000 and 2001 and ending at various times). Coverage is variable.

Lexis Advance provides a database, "North Carolina Legislative Bill History," Documents are selectively included in the database and are vaguely described, such as "Governor's messages" or "Fiscal messages." Stated coverage begins in 2002.

IV. Federal Legislation

Many volumes have been written about the federal legislative process and how to find federal legislative documents. Due to the limited scope of this chapter, the next few pages will provide only a brief overview of the federal legislative process and how it may be researched. The federal legislative process produces extensive documentation at nearly every stage that is freely available online. Due to this fact, engaging in federal legislative research is usually easier than engaging in North Carolina legislative research.

A. Summary of the Federal Legislative Process

The federal legislative process mirrors the process in North Carolina. The federal process is outlined below.[5]

---

5. For a detailed and authoritative explanation of how federal legislation is created see "How Our Laws Are Made," revised and updated by John V. Sullivan, Parliamentarian, United States House of Representatives, House Document 110-49, July 2007, at http://www.gpo.gov/fdsys/pkg/CDOC-110hdoc49.

Federal legislation is created by the introduction of a bill in one of the chambers of the United States Congress, either the House of Representatives or the Senate. The bill is assigned to a committee where deliberations may occur.

In committee, committee staff may prepare a committee print comprising research, documentation, and other information about the subject of the bill. If hearings are held, transcripts of testimony and statements are created. The committee might submit a report reviewing in detail the elements of the bill, the need for the legislation, and a recommendation for passage. Committee reports are usually the most important statement of legislative intent.

If reported favorably by committee, the bill moves to the floor of the chamber for floor debate. Floor debate is transcribed and published in the *Congressional Record*. If the bill is passed by the first chamber, it moves to the second chamber where the process is repeated.

If the second chamber approves the bill in the same form as in the first chamber, the bill is enrolled and sent to the President for signature. If the bill is passed in the second chamber with different amendments, however, then a conference committee must be created to attempt to negotiate the differences. If the conference committee reaches agreement, then the bill is returned to both chambers to be approved and sent to the President for signature.

When presented with a bill passed by Congress, the President may sign the bill into law, ignore the bill (in which case it may become law anyway, depending upon the timing of the legislative session), or veto the bill. If the President signs the bill into law, it becomes a public law and is assigned a public law number such as Pub. L. 111-148. This was the 148th public law passed in the 111th Congress. Public laws are often referred to by popular name. The popular name can be included in the public law itself such as the "The Patient Protection and Affordable Care Act" or can arise through use, such as "Obamacare."

The new public law is issued as a slip law, which is the first publication of a new act passed by the legislature. At the end of the legislative session, the public laws will be compiled and published in chronological order in *Statutes at Large*. Eventually, the Law Revision Council of the United States House of Representatives will codify the new public law into the United States Code.

B. Tracking Current United States Legislation

Researching the current status of federal legislation pending in Congress is a common activity and has benefited greatly from the advent of online access.

1. Using Congress.gov to Track Federal Legislation

The Library of Congress created the Congress.gov[6] website to provide free access to current and archived legislative information. It provides access to bill reports listing a currently updated running record of latest activities concerning each bill. Because so much federal legislative history is available digitally, these running records often link directly to the full text of related documentation, such as committee reports, floor debate as published in the *Congressional Record*, amendments, and recorded votes. Using the bill reports from Congress.gov is the best method of tracking current federal legislation.

The Congress.gov homepage includes a search box in the center of the page for locating bill status by bill number or key words. The retrieved set of bills leads to summaries for each bill, as well as the sponsor, date of introduction, the latest action taken on the bill, any committee reports, and votes.

Selecting one of the tabs along the bottom of the result screen provides more details. The "Summary" tab provides a short explanation of each version of the bill. The "Text" tab will display the text of the most recent version of the bill. You can select a different version of the bill or choose to click on the link to the PDF, which is certified as an official copy by the United States Superintendent of Documents. The "Actions" tab lists all of the actions taken on the bill and can be limited to all (including floor amendments or not) or only major actions. The "Amendments" tab includes proposed changes offered during the legislative process. The "Cosponsors" tab includes every member of Congress who has agreed to sponsor the legislation and the date the sponsorship was made. The "Committees" tab lists all committees and their activity associated with the bill, including committee reports. The "Related Bills" tab includes bills identified by Congress or its staff as similar in subject or related procedurally during the same two-year congressional term.

2. Other Online Sources for Tracking Federal Legislation

Although Congress.gov is the best source for federal bill tracking for legislation enacted since 1995, there are several other options.

---

6. Congress.gov debuted in 2013 and replaces the popular THOMAS platform, which is scheduled to be retired at the end of 2014.

a. Govtrack.us

Use Govtrack.us to receive timely notification via email or RSS of congressional actions on a bill as well as track actions of a member of Congress or the activity of a particular committee. You can track documents that have particular combinations of words, relate to an individual bill number, or affect a U.S. Code section.

b. WestlawNext

WestlawNext has a database for federal bill tracking. It includes summaries and the current status of pending legislation in the United States Congress. Like Congress.gov, this database is updated daily. It is called "Federal Bill Tracking." Historical bill tracking is also available back to 2005 in a database called "Bill Tracking: Historical." Alerts are available in both versions.

c. Lexis Advance

Lexis Advance includes bill tracking information in the "Congressional Bill Tracking" database. Historical running records of bills are found for previous sessions of Congress back to 1989.

d. Bloomberg Law

Bills from the current Congress are available in the "Legislative & Regulatory" tab. Bills from previous Congresses are available back to 1993 in the "Legislative Materials" database. Any search can be set up as an Alert so that new results are delivered by email.

C. Researching Federal Legislative History

1. Why Research Federal Legislative History?

Interpreting statutes is perhaps even more challenging at the federal level where there are often more diverse and competing interests in the legislative process that may affect the final language of legislation. While judges differ in the importance they grant legislative history in interpreting statutes, many courts have relied upon clues to legislative intent that have arisen from the legislative process.

Federal legislative history is also challenging because there are many more documents to consult. Luckily, there are sophisticated tools to help. Remember that a single code section can be the end result of many session laws. To do thorough legislative history research, you must determine which session laws enacted or changed the particular part of code at issue.

2. Shortcuts: Legislative History Available in the Annotated Codes

By using WestlawNext or *West's United States Code Annotated,* you can find references, and sometimes links to the full text, of relevant legislative history documents. For a particular code section, select the "History" tab on West-lawNext. The Editor's and Revisor's notes section of the tab provides a short summary of the changes made by each session law, allowing a researcher to select which session law is relevant. The Legislative History section of the tab provides a list of documents available on WestlawNext for each session law that affected the code section. Currently, Lexis does not integrate legislative history documents into its online or print versions of the U.S. Code.

3. Shortcuts: Compiled Histories

The most important shortcut to researching federal legislative histories is to use a commercially prepared, compiled legislative history. A number of publishers compile and publish complete legislative histories that include all legislative documentation related to a public law. Law libraries collect these publications, and they are usually well indexed. Although there are no free on-line collections of compiled legislative histories, WestlawNext, Lexis Advance, and HeinOnline are increasingly adding compiled legislative histories for major public laws to their online collections in individual databases. For example, WestlawNext has a large collection of compiled legislative histories on a variety of topics in the "U.S. GAO Federal Legislative Histories" database.

4. Shortcuts: Committee Reports

If a compiled legislative history is not available, focus on finding the committee report, which is widely viewed as the most important piece of legislative history. Committee reports are readily available on Congress.gov back to 1995. Selected reports are available back to the 1940s on WestlawNext and 1990 on Lexis Advance.

5. Collecting Your Own Legislative History

Just as in North Carolina, collecting the legislative history of a federal public law is a time consuming task. It is made easier, however, by the superior documentation of the process and the online accessibility of the various types of documentation.

Similar to the process in North Carolina, it is usually easiest to work backwards to collect legislative history documents. The best starting point at the federal level is a statute, preferably from an annotated code. Immediately after the text of the statute in the code, you will find legislative history notes that will include both the *Statutes at Large* and public law citations for the legislation that affected the statute to be researched. In the editor's notes, you may find an explanation of how each session law changed the text of the statute. This can help you determine which session laws affected the portion of the text you are concerned with. Alternatively, you may find the same information by using the Popular Name Table index in any of the United States Code versions, where the popular names of public laws are arranged alphabetically. Beside each popular name is the USC citation, and citations to the public law number and *Statutes at Large* citations for legislation affecting the statute being researched.

Working either online or in print, you may use these citations to find specific, related documents. For example, Congress.gov would be a good source to use for recent committee reports or pages from the *Congressional Record* concerning floor debate.

Two other sources for federal legislative history are ProQuest Congressional and ProQuest Legislative Insight. These databases are powerful tools that have the most comprehensive collection of federal legislative documents. While they are generally accessible only through academic libraries (including law school libraries), they should be consulted when having a complete collection of legislative history documents is important to your legal research and you cannot use Congress.gov or find an already compiled legislative history.

For a summarized comparison of the North Carolina and federal research process and sources, see Table 6-3.

Table 6-3. Comparison of Sources for North Carolina and Federal Legislative History

ACTION	NORTH CAROLINA SOURCES	FEDERAL SOURCES
Pre-Legislative Action	**Study reports** may be produced by ad hoc or standing legislative committees. The reports determine the need for legislation and make recommendations. Reports may be an important source of legislative intent.	
Introduction of Bills	**Bills** are introduced by legislators and published at the General Assembly website (www.ncga.state.nc.us).	**Bills** are introduced by legislators and published at the Government Printing Office's FDsys website (www.gpo.gov/fdsys).
Committee Work	**Minutes** of committee meetings and perhaps exhibits or notes are filed with the Legislative Library. Committees also file less useful form reports, containing only simple recommendations.	**Committee prints** (documentation of related information by committee staffers). **Committee hearings** (transcripts of witness testimony and other statements). **Committee reports** (the most persuasive piece of legislative history).
Floor Debate	*House Journal* records a summary of daily activity and is published at the end of the session. *Senate Journal* records a summary of daily activity and is published at the end of the session.	*Congressional Record* publishes the recorded debates on the floor of the U.S. House and Senate each day.
Session Laws	*North Carolina Session Laws*	*Statutes at Large*
Codified Law	*General Statutes of North Carolina* (official) *West's North Carolina General Statutes Annotated* *General Statutes of North Carolina* (on the General Assembly website).	*United States Code* (official) *United States Code Annotated* *United States Code Service*

Chapter 7

Researching Judicial Opinions

This chapter begins by explaining the state and federal court systems in North Carolina, building on the brief introduction to court systems in Chapter 1. Next the chapter describes the print and online sources of state and federal judicial opinions in North Carolina. The chapter also describes important features of published cases, such as the synopsis and headnotes added by publishers as editorial enhancements. The last half of the chapter addresses how cases may be found in print and online, with a particular focus on finding cases by topic. Searching with terms and connectors (also called Boolean logic) was covered in Chapter 2; those search techniques can also be effective in researching cases.

I. Court Systems

Before the United States of America won its independence and established its own judicial system, it was predominantly a colony of the British crown. The common law judicial system long established in England formed the basis of the judicial system in the American Colonies well before American independence. After American independence, the common law system that had already taken root continued to develop. Many of the original colonies, such as North Carolina, can trace judicial decisions back to the revolutionary war and even earlier than 1776.

A. North Carolina Courts

The current structure of the judicial system in North Carolina is similar to the court structure of other states. The basic structure includes a series of trials courts, an intermediate court of appeals, and a supreme court.

1. Trial Courts in North Carolina

At the trial court level, judges conduct civil and criminal trials. In jury trials generally, the jury determines questions of fact and the presiding judge determines questions of law. In trials without a jury, the judge determines both the facts and the law.

The District Court is the lowest court in North Carolina. Its jurisdiction includes civil cases involving less than $10,000, family law cases, criminal cases involving misdemeanors and infractions, and juvenile cases. Small claims court is a subdivision of the District Court and hears matters involving less than $5,000 where parties are typically not represented by an attorney. The District Court does not entertain jury trials. At least one District Court sits in each of North Carolina's 100 counties, usually in the county seat and typically in a few additional locations in each district.

The Superior Court is the highest trial court in North Carolina. The state's 100 counties are divided into 46 Superior Court districts. Superior Court jurisdiction includes civil cases involving more than $10,000, all felony criminal cases, and misdemeanor criminal cases appealed from a District Court. A 12-member jury hears cases in Superior Court, although juries may be waived. Appeals from North Carolina administrative agency decisions generally are appealed directly to the Superior Court.

Due to the concept of *stare decisis*[1] in the common law system, decisions of higher appellate courts must be followed by lower courts. Trial court decisions, therefore, have little or no precedential value, and are typically not published.

2. North Carolina Court of Appeals

At the North Carolina Court of Appeals, 15 judges typically sit in rotating panels of three. These panels hear practically all cases appealed from the lower District and Superior Courts from across the state. There are a few exceptions. Death penalty cases, for example, are entitled to be appealed directly to the Supreme Court from the Superior Court. The decisions of several specialized North Carolina agencies may be appealed directly to the North Carolina Court of Appeals.

---

1. *Stare decisis* is Latin phrase meaning to "to stand by things decided." In the legal context, *stare decisis* represents the doctrine of precedent requiring courts to follow earlier judicial decisions of a higher court when the same points of law are addressed. *Black's Law Dictionary* (9th ed. 2009).

At this level, the court reviews questions of law but generally does not consider facts that have been determined at the trial court. The Court of Appeals became operational in October 1967, after voters overwhelmingly approved a proposed amendment to Article IV of the North Carolina Constitution. The amendment authorized an intermediate appellate court of appeals to relieve the appellate caseload pressure on the Supreme Court, which until that time handled all trial appeals.

3. North Carolina Supreme Court

Six justices join the Chief Justice to comprise the North Carolina Supreme Court. Like the Court of Appeals, the Supreme Court reviews only questions of law rather than facts, which have already been determined at the trial level.

In several situations, an appellant may appeal to the Supreme Court by right: cases involving constitutional questions; cases from the Court of Appeals that include dissenting opinions; or cases concerning the bar exam, judicial standards, or a utilities commission rate. The Supreme Court may accept an appeal within its discretion in several circumstances, such as a case involving significant public interest or legal principles of major significance.

B. Federal Courts Relevant to North Carolina

The federal judicial system is similar to the three-part structure of North Carolina's judicial system. The federal structure includes a local trial court; an intermediate, regional court of appeals; and the Supreme Court in Washington, D.C. See Appendix B at the back of this book for a map of the geographical boundaries of the federal judicial system.

1. United States District Courts

The federal trial court is the United States District Court, which has original jurisdiction in most federal cases, civil or criminal. The trials may be by jury or bench (judge only). There are 94 federal judicial districts across the country, each with a District Court. Each state has at least one District Court and most states have several. North Carolina has three District Courts: the Western, Middle, and Eastern Districts, with main offices in Charlotte, Greensboro, and Raleigh, N.C., respectively. There are several divisions within each of these three districts.

2. United States Courts of Appeals

The 94 federal districts are organized into 12 regional circuits. Each circuit includes a Court of Appeals serving as the federal, intermediate appellate court for all District Courts that lie in that circuit. North Carolina is in the Fourth Circuit and appeals from the three District Courts in North Carolina are appealed to the Court of Appeals for the Fourth Circuit, based in Richmond, Virginia.

A 13th Court of Appeals, the Court of Appeals for the Federal Circuit, was created with appellate jurisdiction for limited specialized subjects such as patents and certain money claims against the United States government. Appeals of cases concerning these limited subjects from United States District Courts across the country are properly heard in the Court of Appeals for the Federal Circuit.

3. United States Supreme Court

The highest federal court is the Supreme Court, which hears approximately 100 cases a year. The accepted cases may have originated in the federal courts or may have been appealed from a state supreme court. The accepted cases usually involve important U.S. Constitutional law or federal law questions, or instances where U.S. Courts of Appeals from the various circuits have decided the same issue differently, referred to as a *split in the circuits*.

II. Publication of North Carolina Decisions

Because of the importance of previously decided appellate decisions under the concept of *stare decisis*, access to those judicial decisions is critically important to the practice of law. Researchers should understand the historical concept of a reported case. For hundreds of years, individuals rather than corporations were responsible for reporting decisions of the courts. Their work was recorded in books called *reporters*. In the best of circumstances, courts would appoint someone as the reporter for that court's decisions and that person would be responsible for recording and publishing them. When a named individual reported decisions in a book, the book is generically referred to as a *nominative reporter*.

Eventually, courts entered into agreements with publishers who would provide more service than simply reporting what the judge wrote. Publishers began providing editorial enhancements, such as identifying important points of law from each case for indexing purposes. Synopses of the cases were added at the beginning of each case to assist the researcher in quickly understanding what issues the case addressed.

This pattern of publication continues today with corporations taking over the publishing duties. Over 100 years ago, the West Publishing Company began a large scale project of publishing every state's appellate court decisions and providing significant editorial enhancements in regional reporters. There are usually other print reporters, particularly at the state level. Even when working online, researchers are required to cite cases by reporter volumes and page numbers. Therefore, every researcher should understand the concept of reporters and how relevant cases may be located in print and online.

A. Official Reporters

1. *North Carolina Reports*

North Carolina has designated the *North Carolina Reports* as the official reporter of North Carolina Supreme Court decisions. LexisNexis works with North Carolina to publish *North Carolina Reports*. LexisNexis editors analyze each case, identify the points of law from the case, summarize each unique point into a paragraph called a *headnote*, and place those headnotes at the beginning of the case.

2. *North Carolina Court of Appeals Reports*

LexisNexis is also the publisher of the Court of Appeals decisions, in the official *North Carolina Court of Appeals Reports*. As with *North Carolina Reports*, the *Court of Appeals Reports* includes unique headnotes identifying the main points of law at the beginning of each case. The *Court of Appeals Reports* began publication when that court was initiated in 1967.

B. Unofficial Reporters

In addition to the official reporters of North Carolina judicial decisions, there are also unofficial reporters publishing these same cases. In the 1880s, the West Publishing Company (now West, a Thomson Reuters business) began publishing a series of regional reporters. Dividing the nation into regions, each regional reporter set publishes appellate decisions from all the states in that region.

1. *West's South Eastern Reporter*

West's South Eastern Reporter began publication in 1887 and includes the court of appeals and supreme court decisions from the states of North Carolina, Georgia, South Carolina, Virginia, and West Virginia. The *South Eastern Reporter* began when volume 96 of the *North Carolina Reports* was being published. Cases have been duplicated in both reporters since 1887. The value of using the West regional reporter is that the headnotes found at the beginning of each case are connected to the Topic and Key Numbers of the West Digest System. See the discussion about finding cases in Section IV of this chapter.

2. *North Carolina Cases*

A *South Eastern Reporter* offprint, *North Carolina Cases*, contains just the North Carolina decisions taken from the *South Eastern Reporter*. The pagination is identical to *South Eastern Reporter*, so pagination gaps exist in the *North Carolina Cases* where the other states' cases were printed in *South Eastern Reporter*, but not included in *North Carolina Cases*. *North Carolina Cases* might be better suited than the *South Eastern Reporter* to a lawyer only concerned with case law in North Carolina.

C. Features of Reporters

1. Advance Sheets

All hardbound volumes of case reporters, official and unofficial alike, are periodically updated by advance sheet pamphlets. The pamphlets include the cases already prepared with headnotes and the pagination that will exist when the cases are published in the next hardbound volume. Once enough cases have been issued to comprise the next volume, an additional hardbound volume will be published and the associated advance sheets will be removed from the shelf.

2. Tables in Reporters

The reporters have information, often in tabular form, at the beginning or end of each volume. Typically, the tables might include a list of the judges on the bench at the time the opinions in the volume were issued, a list of the cases in the volume arranged in alphabetical order, and some type of subject index. In the *South Eastern Reporter*, all of the cases in each volume have been digested using the Topic and Key Number System to be explained in Section IV.

3. Reporter Series

Reporter publishers often choose to end a series of volume numbers at a particular point, such as volume 200, or volume 999. They will then begin a second series of the reporter. For example, West ended the first series of *South Eastern Reporter* in 1939 and began the second series. A researcher must know the series of the *South Eastern Reporter* along with the volume and page number.

D. Online Fee-based Publication of North Carolina Cases

The publishers listed in Table 7-1 provide access to North Carolina judicial decisions for a fee. Westlaw and Lexis provide the decisions with the most editorial enhancements in addition to the text of the decision. Both are considered the premium services for legal information in the United States. They are generally more expensive than other online services, although there are many subscription pricing options, including the option of buying a document with a credit card. Bloomberg Law provides full access North Carolina judicial decisions but with slightly fewer editorial enhancements. Loislaw provides subscription options that vary from one-day access to an annual subscription. While the coverage of case law is complete, Loislaw provides even fewer editorial enhancements of the text of the cases its databases. VersusLaw and Fastcase are less expensive but with minimal editorial enhancements and less service. Also, VersusLaw and Fastcase provide less extensive coverage for North Carolina case law. All of these companies should provide very quick access to newly issued cases.

Table 7-1. Online Providers of North Carolina Cases

Westlaw

https://lawschool.westlaw.com

"North Carolina Cases" (NC-CS) is a Westlaw database containing North Carolina cases since 1778. It is typically updated within hours or a few days from the issuance of new case law.

LexisNexis

www.lexisnexis.com/lawschool

North Carolina cases can be found in a database with coverage back to 1778. It is typically updated within hours or a few days from the issuance of new case law.

Bloomberg Law

www.bloomberglaw.com

Locate the database from the main page by selecting the "Court Opinions" link and entering "North Carolina" in the "Select Sources" box.

This database contains North Carolina cases since 1778. It is typically updated quickly after the issuance of new case law.

Table 7-1. Online Providers of North Carolina Cases, *cont.*

Fastcase

www.fastcase.com

North Carolina appellate cases are covered back to 1778. While Fastcase is not a free legal research service, the North Carolina Bar Association provides free Fastcase access to Bar Association members. Non-members must still subscribe.

Loislaw

www.loislaw.com

North Carolina appellate cases are covered back to 1778.

VersusLaw

www.versuslaw.com

North Carolina appellate cases are covered back to 1943.

E. Online Free Publication of North Carolina Cases

1. North Carolina Administrative Office of Courts Website

The North Carolina Administrative Office of Courts publishes on its North Carolina Court System website (http://appellate.nccourts.org/opinions/) the slip opinions from the Supreme Court and the Court of Appeals back to 1998. The opinions are posted at least as frequently as once a month. The decisions are posted in reverse chronological order by year. In addition to browsing, the database includes a basic search function. The cases are freely available. However, there are no editorial enhancements such as an editor's synopsis or headnotes at the beginning of the case highlighting the major points of law.

2. North Carolina Cases from Other Websites

Other well known, law-related websites such as Cornell Law School's Legal Information Institute (www.law.cornell.edu) and FindLaw (http://lp.findlaw.com) provide links to North Carolina cases; however, these legal mega-sites simply link directly to the North Carolina Administrative Office of Courts website discussed above, rather than providing a unique database of North Carolina cases.

F. Parts of a Reported Case

Whether in print or online, a reported case will have certain features in common, regardless of the source, whether found in the official reporter, regional reporter, Westlaw, Lexis, Bloomberg Law, one of the lower cost fee-based services, or the court's free website. The actual text of the decision should be identical. Beyond that, however, there may be differences and various levels of enhancements.

To examine and understand some of the various enhancements, see Figure 7-1, a case excerpt from *South Eastern Reporter*, and Figure 7-2, an excerpt from the same case as displayed in WestlawNext.

Figure 7-1. Example of a North Carolina Supreme Court Case Viewed in West's *South Eastern Reporter*

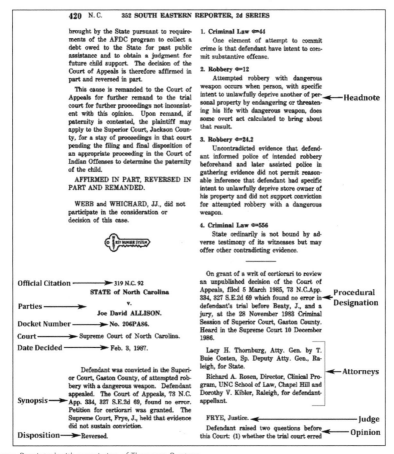

Source: Reprinted with permission of Thomson-Reuters.

Figure 7-2. Example of the Same North Carolina Supreme Court Case Viewed in WestlawNext

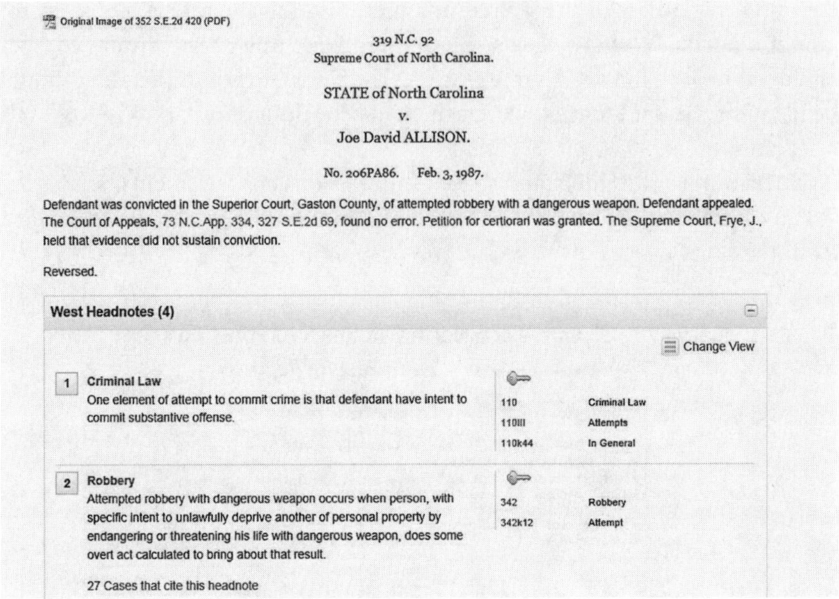
Original Image of 352 S.E.2d 420 (PDF)

319 N.C. 92
Supreme Court of North Carolina.

STATE of North Carolina
v.
Joe David ALLISON.

No. 206PA86. Feb. 3, 1987.

Defendant was convicted in the Superior Court, Gaston County, of attempted robbery with a dangerous weapon. Defendant appealed. The Court of Appeals, 73 N.C.App. 334, 327 S.E.2d 69, found no error. Petition for certiorari was granted. The Supreme Court, Frye, J., held that evidence did not sustain conviction.

Reversed.

West Headnotes (4)

Change View

1 Criminal Law
One element of attempt to commit crime is that defendant have intent to commit substantive offense.

110 Criminal Law
110III Attempts
110k44 In General

2 Robbery
Attempted robbery with dangerous weapon occurs when person, with specific intent to unlawfully deprive another of personal property by endangering or threatening his life with dangerous weapon, does some overt act calculated to bring about that result.

342 Robbery
342k12 Attempt

27 Cases that cite this headnote

Source: Reprinted with permission of Thomson-Reuters.

Parallel Citations. The cases in most jurisdictions are published in more than one print reporter. For example, North Carolina Supreme Court decisions are reported in *North Carolina Reports* and *South Eastern Reporter*. While the text of the decision is identical, the editorial enhancements will be different. Cases reported *in South Eastern Reporter* include the parallel citation to where the case may be found in the official reporter as well.

Parties and Procedural Designations. The parties involved in the litigation are listed at the beginning of the case. Procedural designations such as appellant and appellee, may also be included by some editors.

Docket Number. Each court assigns a unique number to a case when it is filed with the court. The number is used much like a name, organizing, identifying, and locating documents related to the case.

Court and Date. The court issuing the opinion and the date of the opinion are listed.

Synopsis. One of the significant editorial enhancements provided by publishers is a synopsis of the case. The synopsis usually summarizes the facts, the procedural position of the case, the important legal issues involved, and the disposition. A synopsis will aid the researcher by providing a quick overview to determine the relevancy of the legal issues involved in the case and whether time should be spent reading the case. Sometimes the court's own decision will include a synopsis by the justice writing the opinion. Although perhaps not as user-friendly as an editorial version, the court-written synopsis would be available in an opinion posted from a free court website. Freely accessible cases otherwise do not have a synopsis.

Disposition. A court's ultimate decision, the disposition, is often stated immediately after the synopsis in a reported case. The court may decide to affirm the lower court's ruling. However, if the appellate court disagrees, it may decide to reverse, remand, or vacate the decision. Occasionally, a court may agree with only part of a lower court's decision. In that situation the court will affirm in part and reverse in part.

Headnotes. Each case involves at least one legal issue and often several. When accessing a case from a print reporter, Westlaw, or Lexis, you will note that editors provide a short paragraph setting out each point of law from the case and arrange the paragraphs at the beginning of the case. Containing more detail than the synopsis, these headnotes provide a quick window into the various legal issues involved in the case. Some publishers use the exact language from the text of the case in the headnote. Other publishers standardize the language in the headnote, using words that are more generic and likely to also appear in other similar cases. Each headnote begins with a number. Locating that number in the text of the opinion identifies the part of the opinion discussing that point of law. In online services such as Westlaw or Lexis, these numbers are hypertextlinked to the relevant part of the case where that point of law is discussed.

Headnote captions may be linked to some type of case-finding index or digest. The best known of these is West's Topic and Key Number Digest System, which is available in print as well as on Westlaw. See Section IV for more information. The headnotes from North Carolina cases reported in the *South Eastern Reporter* are part of the West Topic and Key Number Digest System.

Opinion. Following all of the editorial enhancements is the text of the court's opinion. Before a case is useful for any purpose in the practice of law, the researcher must read the actual text of the opinion. If the decision is not unanimous, a case may have more than one opinion. Several possible decisions include the following: a majority opinion, where a majority of judges are in agreement; a concurring opinion, where one or more judges agree with the outcome of the majority but not the reasoning; or a dissenting opinion, in which a judge disagrees with the majority's outcome. The majority opinion becomes binding precedent. At some future time, a well-crafted dissenting opinion may become useful as an artful statement of the opposing view or for litigants hoping to reverse the majority opinion. If there is no majority agreement on the reasoning of a decision, but a majority of judges reaches the same outcome, the court's decision is a plurality decision.

G. Published vs. Unpublished

Appellate judges in most jurisdictions are allowed to determine the precedential value of each case they decide. They may decide that a case lacks precedential value and is not worth publishing in a reporter. That case is designated as an unpublished case. Unpublished cases are treated differently in various jurisdictions, and the jurisdictional rule is usually determined by that jurisdiction's appellate court rules.

In North Carolina, Rules of Appellate Procedure, Rule 30(e)(3) states, "An unpublished decision of the North Carolina Court of Appeals does not constitute controlling legal authority." The rule further states that the citation to unpublished opinions in North Carolina trial or appellate courts is "disfavored." However, "[i]f a party believes, nevertheless, that an unpublished opinion has precedential value to a material issue in the case and that there is no published opinion that would serve as well, the party may cite the unpublished opinion...." The citing party must disclose that the opinion is unpublished and serve a copy on all parties. The judge ultimately decides the value of the precedent to the case being litigated.

III. Publication of Other States' Judicial Opinions

While other states' judicial opinions are not mandatory authority in North Carolina, they may be persuasive, particularly when a legal issue has not been addressed by North Carolina courts. Thus, a researcher may need to find other state's cases on occasion. Fortunately, once a researcher gains an understanding of the print and online publication pattern for North Carolina cases, other states' publication patterns are easily understood.

The names and designation of official print reporters for each state are listed in "Appendix 1: Primary Sources by Jurisdiction" of the *ALWD Guide* and in "Table T.1: United States Jurisdictions" in the *Bluebook*. Often, the nearby states' cases are included in the same regional reporter. For example, *South Eastern Reporter,* which contains the North Carolina appellate cases, also contains the cases of Georgia, South Carolina, Virginia, and West Virginia. With a few exceptions, each state's appellate court decisions designated for publication will be included in one of the regional reporters.[2] See Table 7-2 for a list of the West regional reporters and the states covered by each.

Table 7-2. West's Regional Reporters and States Included

Atlantic Reporter (A., A.2d)	Connecticut, Delaware, District of Columbia, Maine Maryland, New Hampshire, New Jersey, Pennsylvania, Rhode Island, and Vermont
North Eastern Reporter (N.E., N.E.2d)	Illinois, Indiana, Massachusetts, New York, and Ohio
North Western Reporter (N.W., N.W.2d)	Iowa, Michigan, Minnesota, Nebraska, North Dakota, South Dakota, and Wisconsin
Pacific Reporter (P., P.2d, P.3d)	Alaska, Arizona, California, Colorado, kansas, Montana, Nevada, New Mexico, Oklahoma, Oregon, Utah, Washington, and Wyoming
South Eastern Reporter (S.E., S.E.2d)	Georgia, North Carolina, South Carolina, Virginia, and West Virginia
South Western Reporter (S.W., S.W.2d)	Arkansas, Kentucky, Missouri, Tennessee, and Texas
Southern Reporter (So., So. 2d, So. 3d)	Alabama, Florida, Louisiana, and Mississippi

Online cases from other states are even easier to locate since the researcher does not have to know the name of the print reporter. Like North Carolina cases, other states' cases are published at each state's court website, and from

---

2. Although *North Eastern Reporter* is designated for New York appellate cases, the intermediate appellate court decisions are not included. Instead, they have been included in a separate West reporter called *New York Supplement* since the late 1800s. New York's ultimate appellate court decisions, however, are published in *North Eastern Reporter*. Similarly, the opinions of California's intermediate appellate court have been published in a separate West reporter, *California Reporter*, rather than the *Pacific Reporter*, since 1960.

one of the online services such as Westlaw, Lexis, Bloomberg, Loislaw, Fastcase, or VersusLaw.

IV. Publication of Federal Court Decisions

A. Print Publications

Federal cases are primarily published by private publishers. See Table 7-3 for an overview of the courts and the names of the reporters publishing their cases.

Table 7-3. Reporters for Federal Court Cases

Court	Reporter Name	Abbreviations
U.S. Supreme Court	*United States Reports* (official)	U.S.
	Supreme Court Reporter	S. Ct.
	United States Supreme Court Reports, Lawyers' Edition	L. Ed., L. Ed. 2d
U.S. Courts of Appeals	*Federal Reporter*, 1880	F., F.2d, F.3d
	Federal Cases, 1789–1879	F. Cas
	Federal Appendix, 2001–	F. App.
U.S. District Courts	*Federal Supplement*, 1932–	F. Supp., F. Supp. 2d
	Federal Rules Decisions, 1940– (limited coverage)	F.R.D.

1. Reporters for Federal Cases

a. Federal Supplement

U.S. District Court opinions have been published by West in the *Federal Supplement* since the beginning of the reporter in 1932. Although the government has not designated a reporter as an official government reporter of federal District Court opinions, this reporter is used and cited in courts. Selected District Court opinions from all over the country, including North Carolina's three federal District Courts when designated for publication, are reported chronologically in the *Federal Supplement*. The following list shows the dates of coverage by series:

Federal Supplement, 2d   1998–

Federal Supplement   1932–1998

b. Federal Rules Decisions

The *Federal Rules Decisions* is a West reporter of U.S. District Court decisions strictly limited to those decisions addressing cases construing Federal Rules of Civil Procedure, the Federal Rules of Criminal Procedure, the Federal Rules of Appellate Procedure, and the Federal Rules of Evidence, that are not reported in *Federal Supplement*.

c. Federal Reporter

The majority of U.S. Court of Appeals decisions are designated for publication in the Federal Reporter. (Those that are not so designated have been published in the *Federal Appendix* since 2001.) Researchers interested in U.S. Court of Appeals decisions affecting North Carolina would find opinions from the Court of Appeals for the Fourth Circuit in this reporter. *Federal Reporter* is another unofficial West reporter and began publication in 1880. The following list shows the dates of coverage by series:

Federal Reporter, 3d   1993–

Federal Reporter, 2d   1925–1993

Federal Reporter   1880–1925

d. Federal Appendix

Published since 2001, this unofficial West reporter includes cases from the U.S. Court of Appeals that were not designated for publication in the Federal Reporter and are therefore "unpublished."

e. Federal Cases

Federal Cases is a collection of 30 volumes and a digest reporting U.S. Circuit Court decisions "from the earliest times to the beginning of the federal reporter." Coverage dates are 1789 to 1879. The set was published between 1894 and 1897 by West.

f. United States Reports

The official reporter of Supreme Court decisions, *United States Reports* is published by the Government Printing Office. It is a notoriously slow publication. Due to the fact that it is at least three or four years behind at this writing, and offers no particular editorial enhancements, it is rarely used for practical purposes or purposes that require recent information. As it is the official version, however, most citation rules require citation to *United States Reports*, if it is available.

Early in the Court's history, there was no official reporter of the decisions. The first volumes were privately reported (nominative reporters) and still bear the names of the reporters, such as Dallas, Cranch, and Wheaton, even though they have now been incorporated into *United States Reports.*

g. United States Supreme Court Reports, Lawyers' Edition

The *United States Supreme Court Reports, Lawyers' Edition* is a privately published reporter that provides complete coverage of United States Supreme Court decisions. Now published by LexisNexis, the reporter has traditionally offered editorial enhancements such as summaries of briefs submitted to the court and articles written by editorial staff addressing the legal topics from the decision for selected cases.

h. West's Supreme Court Reporter

Published by West, the *Supreme Court Reporter* began coverage of United States Supreme Court decisions in 1882. The cases include traditional West enhancements such as headnotes connected to the West Topic and Key Number Digest System.

2. Advance Sheets

Just as discussed with the state court reporters, U.S. print reporters for federal cases are updated in the same manner. Within four to six weeks of a decision, federal cases selected for publication are issued in pamphlets known as advance sheets. Those Court of Appeals decisions not selected for publication might be selected for the *Federal Appendix* and would appear in advance sheets for that reporter. Eventually, cases published in advance sheets are incorporated in a new volume of the reporter, and the advance sheets are discarded.

B. Online Publication

The same publishers listed in Table 7-1 as providing access to North Carolina cases, also provide access to federal judicial decisions for a fee. Of those fee-based providers, only VersusLaw does not provide comprehensive coverage of federal cases in North Carolina.

C. Free Online Federal Cases

The websites of each of the United States District Courts in North Carolina (Western District at www.ncwd.uscourts.gov, Middle District at www.ncmd.us courts.gov, and Eastern District at www.nced.uscourts.gov) link to recent decisions from the court. These decisions are in the nature of slip opinions. They are free but lack any editorial enhancements and usually represent a selected collection of recent decisions. If the decisions are not posted on the court's website, the link might connect to PACER, the federal "Public Access to Court Electronic Records" website (http://www.pacer.gov) where court documents can be downloaded for a minimal charge.

The United States Court of Appeals for the Fourth Circuit also frequently posts its decisions in PDF format at the court's website (www.ca4.uscourts.gov).

The United States Supreme Court frequently posts copies of its decisions in PDF format at the Court's website (www.supremecourtus.gov).

D. Published vs. Unpublished

Federal cases may be designated either published or unpublished, just like state cases, depending upon a judge's disposition of the potential precedential value. A small number of federal District Court (trial court) decisions are published. A majority of federal Court of Appeals decisions are published. All United States Supreme Court decisions are published. However, unpublished decisions have been distributed for years and are widely available online.

Prior to 2007, the rules in the various federal circuits treated the issue of the use of unreported decisions differently. Some circuits prohibited the citation of unpublished opinions and some circuits allowed it. The question was settled in December 2006 when the Federal Rules of Appellate Procedure were amended to add Rule 32.1. The new rule provides that a federal court may not prohibit or restrict the citation of federal judicial opinions that have been designated as unpublished and issued on or after January 1, 2007. If the decision is not available in a publically accessible electronic database, the citing party must file a copy with the court and serve a copy to the parties. As with the North Carolina rule, the federal rule did not address what weight the court must give the unpublished decision.

V. Finding Cases Using Print Resources

The easiest way to find a case is to use a known citation. Researchers are rarely so lucky! The next recommended method of case-finding is to spend a few minutes researching a topic in secondary sources such as an encyclopedia, a treatise discussing a specific subject (especially one focused on the relevant jurisdiction), or an *American Law Reports* annotation. These secondary sources will assist in several ways. First, they might provide citations to relevant cases. Alternatively, reading relevant background information will assist you in selecting more specific and relevant search terms for a better search, either in print or online. For more about secondary sources, see Chapter 3.

The focus of the remainder of this chapter is the use of specific tools or strategies to locate cases without a known citation. Using print resources, the best tool is a digest of cases.

A. Digests

Digests are multi-volume indexes of case summaries from a specific jurisdiction arranged by subject. The best known and most widely available case law digest is the West Digest System. West digests are available in practically every jurisdiction, both state and federal. Therefore, learning to use them enables a researcher to use a West digest from any jurisdiction to research cases. West publishes the *North Carolina Digest*. Understanding what print digests are and how they are created is important even if you never pick up a single volume of a print digest. The digest system is available through Westlaw and is an essential component of WestlawNext's sophisticated Global Search process.

The concept of a case law digest is relatively simple. First, an outline of American law was created. West selected just over 400 legal subjects as digest "Topics." Topics may be broad subject areas of law such as "Criminal Law" or narrower subject areas such as "Good Will." Within each Topic is an extensive set of subdivisions called "Key Numbers" representing every conceivable legal issue under that Topic. This outline incorporates and organizes the points of law into a reasonably logical arrangement. While the system is not perfect, it works well. It also becomes easier to use, and can be used more effectively, the more familiar you become with the Topics and Key Number System. Although law is constantly changing, this basic outline of American law used in all West digests has been in place for over 100 years.

The second, and ongoing, component in a digest system is the linking of all the Topics and Key Numbers in the system to cases in your jurisdiction addressing those specific points of law. The result is the classification of every case from your jurisdiction into a subject matter arrangement.

1. Headnotes

Editors read every case and identify points of law from each case. The editors write a headnote, a summarizing paragraph from the case concerning that point of law, for each identified point of law in the case. Some publishers use the exact language directly from the case as the language for the headnote. The West editors, however, standardize the language of the headnote, using more common language that is more likely to be found in similar cases. For keyword searching online, this standardized language from the headnotes in the database may provide a significant advantage.

2. Topics and Key Numbers, and Their Relationship to Headnotes

The editors assign each of the headnotes in a case a Topic and Key Number from the West Digest System. The Topic, Key Number, and headnotes are published at the beginning of each case in the case reporter and may be used by researchers to quickly grasp what the case is about and whether it is relevant enough to read the entire case.

Each headnote from each case is also added to the digest in the appropriate location under a Topic and Key Number. When the researcher finds the appropriate Topic and Key Number, she will find right beneath it all the headnotes from all the cases that address that legal issue. Under each Topic and Key Number, the headnotes are listed in the hierarchical order of the courts in that jurisdiction. For example, in the *North Carolina Digest*, cases would be listed first from the Supreme Court, then the Court of Appeals. Each of the headnotes listed in the digest includes a case name and reporter citation. You can easily move from the headnotes in the digest to the reporter (print or online) using the citation. See Figure 7-3 for an example of a page from the *North Carolina Digest*.

One of the useful features of the digest system is that the Topics and Key Numbers are consistent throughout all jurisdictions in the United States. Once a researcher finds the relevant Topic and Key Number(s) for her research, she can go to the digest for any jurisdiction, state or federal, and find cases addressing that legal issue.

To assist in finding cases in the West regional reporters, West publishes four regional digests: Atlantic Digest, North Western Digest, Pacific Digest, and South Eastern Digest. In addition, West publishes some state digests. Attorneys researching North Carolina cases would use either *South Eastern Digest* or *North Carolina Digest*.

B. Methods of Using Digests

There are several methods of using the digest to find cases relevant to a specific topic being researched. These methods will be discussed below in turn.

Figure 7-3. Example from West's *North Carolina Digest*

34 N C D 2d—71   ROBBERY ☞12

For references to other topics, see Descriptive-Word Index

N.C.App. 1972. Fact that defendant failed to obtain any money from victim did not preclude conviction of armed robbery.

State v. Kinsey, 193 S.E.2d 430, 17 N.C.App. 57, certiorari denied 194 S.E.2d 153, 282 N.C. 674.

N.C.App. 1972. Statute proscribing robbery with a dangerous weapon creates no new offense; the only distinctions between common-law robbery and armed robbery under the statute are whether the life of the person robbed is endangered or threatened by the weapon, and the more severe punishment which may be imposed for armed robbery. G.S. § 14–87.

State v. Osborne, 185 S.E.2d 593, 13 N.C.App. 420.

N.C.App. 1969. Actual possession and use or threatened use by defendants of firearms or other dangerous weapon are necessary to constitute offense of robbery with firearms or other dangerous weapon. G.S. § 14–87.

State v. Faulkner, 168 S.E.2d 9, 5 N.C.App. 113.

N.C.App. 1968. Where witness first saw defendant standing at counter of store with gun in his hand and defendant placed gun on counter in front of him and demanded that witness give him money, defendant sufficiently used or threatened use of firearm as charged in indictment for armed robbery. G.S. § 14–87.

State v. Green, 162 S.E.2d 641, 2 N.C.App. 170.

☞**12. Attempt.**

Library references

C.J.S. Robbery §§ 78–80, 82.

N.C. 1996. "Attempted robbery with dangerous weapon" occurs when person, with specific intent to unlawfully deprive another of personal property by endangering or threatening his life with dangerous weapon, does some overt act calculated to bring about this result.

State v. Miller, 477 S.E.2d 915, 344 N.C. 658.

Shooting gun at someone may be sufficient overt act to support charge of attempted robbery, when accompanied by evidence of intent to rob victim.

State v. Miller, 477 S.E.2d 915, 344 N.C. 658.

Juvenile defendant had already committed overt act in furtherance of crime of robbery well before he left the scene, by placing his hand on pistol to withdraw it with intent of shooting and robbing victim, and thus he did not legally abandon his plan to commit armed robbery as would preclude attempted robbery conviction, even though he did not take victim's money.

State v. Miller, 477 S.E.2d 915, 344 N.C. 658.

N.C. 1996. Attempted robbery with a dangerous weapon is the unlawful attempt to take personal property from another or in another's presence by use or threatened use of firearm or other dangerous weapon which threatens or endangers the life of another. G.S. § 14–87(a).

State v. Workman, 476 S.E.2d 301, 344 N.C. 482.

N.C. 1995. Two elements of attempted robbery with a dangerous weapon are (1) intent to commit substantive offense, and (2) overt act done for that purpose which goes beyond mere preparation but falls short of completed offense. G.S. § 14–87.

State v. Davis, 455 S.E.2d 627, 340 N.C. 1, certiorari denied 116 S.Ct. 136, 516 U.S. 846, 133 L.Ed.2d 83, certiorari denied Hood v. North Carolina, 116 S.Ct. 136, 516 U.S. 846, 133 L.Ed.2d 83.

N.C. 1994. That things did not go exactly as planned between two defendants such that defendants did not actually take drugs from victim did not negate attempted armed robbery conviction.

State v. Bell, 450 S.E.2d 710, 338 N.C. 363, certiorari denied 115 S.Ct. 2619, 515 U.S. 1163, 132 L.Ed.2d 861.

N.C. 1994. To establish robbery or attempted robbery with dangerous weapon, state is required to prove beyond reasonable doubt that defendant possessed firearm or other dangerous weapon at time of robbery or attempted robbery and that victim's life was in danger or threatened. G.S. § 14–87.

State v. Williams, 438 S.E.2d 727, 335 N.C. 518.

N.C. 1993. Attempt to take illegal drugs and money from sale of illegal drugs could be basis for conviction of attempted armed robbery and for conviction of first-degree murder under felony-murder rule.

State v. Oliver, 434 S.E.2d 202, 334 N.C. 513.

N.C. 1991. Attempted armed robbery is unlawful attempt at taking of personal property from another by use of firearm or other dangerous weapon.

State v. McDowell, 407 S.E.2d 200, 329 N.C. 363.

N.C. 1987. Attempted robbery with dangerous weapon occurs when person, with specific intent to unlawfully deprive another of personal property by endangering or threatening his life with dangerous weapon, does some overt act calculated to bring about that result.

State v. Allison, 352 S.E.2d 420, 319 N.C. 92.

N.C. 1981. An attempted armed robbery occurs when person with requisite intent does

Source: Reprinted with permission of Thomson-Reuters.

The best method will always depend upon what information the researcher already has when approaching the digest.

1. The "One Good Case" Method

Occasionally, a researcher will begin a project with a known, relevant case in hand. For example, a more experienced attorney may suggest that you look at the "Smith" case from several years ago before starting your case law research because she thinks it might be relevant. If you have one good case with a headnote that addresses the issue on point, simply note the Topic and Key Number at the top of the headnote. Look at the other headnotes listed under that Topic and Key Number in the digest to find a list of all the relevant cases addressing that legal issue in that jurisdiction. This is perhaps the easiest way of using the digest.

2. Descriptive-Word Index Method

Typically, however, the researcher won't be starting with a case already in hand. Rather, the starting point will simply be a legal topic. In that situation, the best starting point will likely be the "Descriptive-Word Index." The purpose of the Descriptive-Word Index is to connect your search terms with related Topics and Key Numbers in the digest, and more importantly, the headnotes listed under the Key Numbers.

First, generate search terms, as addressed in Chapter 2. Of course, the more specific and relevant your search terms, the easier it will be to connect with relevant Topics and Key Numbers in the digest. Next, search the Descriptive-Word Index in the digest for the jurisdiction being researched. The index is arranged alphabetically. Look up each search term in the index and record the Topics and Key Numbers that are found. Be sure to check the pocket part of each volume of the Descriptive-Word Index, too. If you encounter challenges in finding your search terms, return to secondary sources such as a legal encyclopedia, subject-specific treatise, or a law journal to get more background information about the legal issue being researched. This approach will assist with the development of relevant search terms. Returning to the Descriptive-Word Index after increasing background knowledge is often more productive.

The next step is to move from the Descriptive-Word Index to the main volumes of the digest to begin checking the specific Topics and Key Numbers identified from the Descriptive-Word Index. The Topics are printed on the spine of the volumes and are arranged throughout the digest set in alphabetical order. Select the Topic volume and find the Key Number in the Topic in the volume. After locating the Topic, quickly browse the information at the beginning of the Topic that describes the legal subjects covered by that Topic. Another section, "Subjects Excluded and Covered by Other Topics," might also be useful. Under the Topic heading is a table of contents of all the Key Numbers for that Topic, referred to as "Analysis" or "Topic Analysis." If there is an extensive number of Key Numbers, there may be a summary table of contents, and then the more detailed table of contents that includes all the Key Numbers. You may benefit from browsing the Analysis to see where the Key Numbers you identified from the index fit within the larger framework of the Topic. Additional relevant Key Numbers may be found through this process.

Look at each of the Key Numbers identified from the index and read the case headnotes. Record the case name and citation to any case that appears relevant and worth reading based upon review of the headnote. Although this process might seem repetitive, dull, or monotonous, it is critically important to the outcome of the research. Careful and thorough review of the Key Numbers and headnotes will provide more certainty when conclusions are drawn and client decisions are made at the end of the research project.

The attorney researching a legal issue with a particular outcome in mind must be able to read the headnotes and related cases objectively and not fear cases that suggest an unfavorable outcome. Be certain that the opposing attorney will find and use these cases to their greatest benefit. Those cases are often the most important ones and are certainly cases that need to be identified and addressed in the research and lawyering process. For example, can a case that is clear but "bad" for a particular viewpoint be distinguished? If not, would the client have an alternative legal theory? This is part of the art of practicing law.

The next step in the case research process using digests is to update the information from the Topic volume. This process has several layers: check the volume's pocket part for the same Topic and Key Numbers; look for a freestanding paperback supplement to that volume, usually housed adjacent to the volume; and search for a cumulative supplementary pamphlet (perhaps quarterly or semi-annually) for the full digest. These pamphlets are usually shelved at the end of the digest set and should be checked if available. The outside cover of any pamphlet should note the applicable dates of coverage.[3]

---

3. Even the cumulative supplementary pamphlets may be updated. Note the "most recent case included in this pamphlet" information from the cumulative supplementary pamphlet. This will tell you the volume and page number of the reporter containing the last case included in the cumulative supplementary pamphlet. Recall that each reporter volume of any West reporter set, such as *South Eastern Reporter*, includes a

3. Topic Analysis or Outline Method

When a researcher has researched a legal issue numerous times or developed an understanding of how to use a digest, she may want to try the "Topic Analysis Method" or "Outline Approach." This approach involves selecting the appropriate Topic volume from the shelf (by-passing the Descriptive-Word Index) and examining the Topic Analysis or Outline and finding relevant Key Numbers.

The danger with this method is that the researcher might entirely miss non-intuitive Topics that have relevant Key Numbers. The Descriptive-Word Index is designed to prevent that from happening; however, if an attorney practices criminal law for example, and has practiced for some time using the digest to find case law, she might be in a position to work directly from the "Criminal Law" Topic.

4. Table of Cases Method

Occasionally, a researcher will know the name of one of the parties to a case (plaintiff or defendant) but not the citation. This situation might arise when an assigning partner or co-worker mentions the name of a case that is possibly relevant. The Table of Cases at the end of the digest set provides a list of all the cases in the digest arranged alphabetically by plaintiff and defendant. Use of the "Table of Cases" might facilitate the "One Good Case" method described above.

An alternative use of the Table of Cases is to transition from a reported case that lacks the West Topic and Key Numbers, such as the *North Carolina Supreme Court Reports*, to a West digest, such as the *North Carolina Digest*. The researcher may look up the case in the Table of Cases of the *North Carolina Digest*, using the case name, and find the Topics and Key Numbers associated with that case. From the Table of Cases, the researcher may move to the Topic volume to find relevant headnotes from like cases under the Key Number.

---

miniature digest of the cases included in the volume. Find the reporter volume identified by the cumulative supplementary pamphlet and look up your Topic and Key Numbers in that individual volume's digest to find any relevant cases in that volume. Do this for each subsequent volume. Then, follow this same procedure for each advance sheet pamphlet issued for that reporter set. This process will ultimately bring you up to approximately several weeks from the present time. To be more current beyond the most recent advance sheet digests, you must go online.

5. Words and Phrases Method

Words that have been judicially defined, and the cases defining them, may be found for a specific jurisdiction using the Words and Phrases part of the digest. Obviously, a judicially defined word or phrase is useful for a common law legal subject where there are no applicable statutory definitions. A judicial definition of a term is superior to a generic legal dictionary definition since the judicial definition is more specific to the relevant jurisdiction. Also, judicially defined terms are useful when interpreting statutory law that may include vague terms or terms not defined in the statute. Another useful feature of a "Words and Phrases" entry is a list of the relevant Topics and Key Numbers used for headnotes in the case that defined the term.

VI. Finding Cases Online

There are many methods of finding cases online. Chapter 2 dealt with basic online searching issues such as full-text searching, keyword searching, and field (or segment) searching. This chapter will address finding cases by subject using some of the tools available using WestlawNext, Lexis Advance, and Bloomberg Law, beyond the simple terms and connector searching that is available with any online database service with less sophisticated search options such as Loislaw, Fastcase, VersusLaw, etc.

A. West's Key Number Digest Online

1. Initiating a Search using the West Key Number System

The human-added value of classifying all of American case law by subject into an index system is also available online in WestlawNext. To access this classification system online as a starting point for case searching, select the "Tools" tab on the main page under the universal search bar. Next, select the "West Key Number System" link to access the Key Number Digest page.

The first option at the Key Number Digest page is to select a jurisdiction, such as North Carolina, and then enter a search in the search bar. This option searches the text of all the Topics and headnotes in the digest of cases from the selected jurisdiction. To add context to the retrieved results, the results include a fragment of the outline of the digest where that Topic and Key Number are classified.

Another obvious option is to simply browse the Topics and Key Numbers for relevant cases. This option allows you to browse all 400+ Topics, breaking them out by Key Number headings and eventually by headnotes where individual cases under a specific Key Number may be viewed. See Figure 7-4 for a view of browsing the list of Topics and Key Numbers on WestlawNext.

Figure 7-4. Browsing the List of Topics and Key Numbers on WestlawNext

WestlawNext	Q ⌄ Search West Key Number System		North Carolina ▼

Home

👉 **West Key Number System** ☆ Add to Favorites

☐ Select all content | 0 items selected

○ Search all content ◉ Specify content to searc

☐1	ABANDONED AND LOST PROPERTY	☐136	DOWER AND CURTESY	☐285	PARENT AND CHILD
☐2	ABATEMENT AND REVIVAL	☐141	EASEMENTS	☐286	PARLIAMENTARY LAW
☐4	ABORTION AND BIRTH CONTROL	☐141E	EDUCATION	☐287	PARTIES
☐5	ABSENTEES	☐142	EJECTMENT	☐288	PARTITION
☐6	ABSTRACTS OF TITLE	☐142T	ELECTION LAW	☐289	PARTNERSHIP
☐7	ACCESSION	☐143	ELECTION OF REMEDIES	☐290	PARTY WALLS
☐8	ACCORD AND SATISFACTION	☐145	ELECTRICITY	☐291	PATENTS
☐9	ACCOUNT	☐146	EMBEZZLEMENT	☐294	PAYMENT
☐10	ACCOUNT, ACTION ON	☐148	EMINENT DOMAIN	☐295	PENALTIES
☐11	ACCOUNT STATED	☐149	ENTRY, WRIT OF	☐296	PENSIONS
☐11A	ACCOUNTANTS	☐149E	ENVIRONMENTAL LAW	☐297	PERJURY
☐12	ACKNOWLEDGMENT	☐149T	EQUITABLE CONVERSION	☐298	PERPETUITIES
☐13	ACTION	☐150	EQUITY	☐300	PILOTS
☐14	ACTION ON THE CASE	☐151	ESCAPE	☐302	PLEADING
☐15	ADJOINING LANDOWNERS	☐152	ESCHEAT	☐303	PLEDGES
☐15A	ADMINISTRATIVE LAW AND PROCEDURE	☐154	ESTATES IN PROPERTY	☐305	POSSESSORY WARRANT
		☐156	ESTOPPEL	☐306	POSTAL SERVICE
☐16	ADMIRALTY	☐157	EVIDENCE	☐307	POWERS
☐17	ADOPTION	☐158	EXCEPTIONS, BILL OF	☐307A	PRETRIAL PROCEDURE
☐18	ADULTERATION	☐159	EXCHANGE OF PROPERTY	☐308	PRINCIPAL AND AGENT
☐19	ADULTERY	☐160	EXCHANGES	☐309	PRINCIPAL AND SURETY
		☐161	EXECUTION	☐310	PRISONS

Source: Reprinted with permission of Thomson-Reuters.

Note that on WestlawNext, the Topics have also been assigned numbers, which display in the digest list of Topics. The Topic may be represented by either the Topic name or its number before the "K" (or key symbol) and the Key Number follows. Browsing the list of Topics on Westlaw is somewhat akin to the Topic Analysis or Outline approach discussed above using print digests. The additional value, however, is that you may create a more restrictive search by identifying a discrete portion of the digest and searching that portion with your own relevant keywords.

2. Working from a Retrieved Case on the Screen

Another way to access the digest online is to select a Topic and Key Number from a relevant headnote of a retrieved case displaying on WestlawNext. You are presented with a list of all the cases under that Topic and Key Number from that case's jurisdiction. Options include changing the jurisdiction to find cases from other courts addressing that point of law.

3. Using a Topic and Key Number to Create a Search in a Database

Using a known Topic and Key Number, you may select any jurisdiction from the universal search bar at the main WestlawNext page and enter the Topic and Key Number as a search term without going through the West Key Number System page. As mentioned earlier, Topic names are also assigned a unique number. Using a Topic and Key number as a search term requires that you use the Topic number instead of the Topic name, along with the Key Number. For example, the Topic "Adoption," which is given the Topic number 17 on WestlawNext, and Key Number 5, "Persons who may be adopted," would be entered as 17K5 with no spaces. WestlawNext recognizes the number 17 as the Topic "Adoption" and the letter "K" instructs the search software that this is a Topic and Key Number search within the database.

B. Searching in WestlawNext's Practice Areas

Another method of subject searching on WestlawNext is to select a database that has already been limited to cases concerning a particular subject. One of the best practices of full-text, keyword searching is to begin with the smallest database that will have all of the relevant cases. A topical database within the specific judicial jurisdiction should satisfy that goal. From the main WestlawNext screen, select the "Practice Areas" tab below the universal search bar. These databases contain more than state cases in each topical area; for example, a database might contain statutes, law review articles, current news, and federal cases. Some topical areas may be limited to a database of all states' cases on the Topic, but many can be narrowed to a particular state. However, some coverage may vary by state. Therefore, a researcher may not know whether her search of a particular jurisdiction through a practice area database is comprehensive.

To search for North Carolina cases about family law, begin by selecting "Family Law" from the "Practice Areas" page. Next select "Family Law Cases." You will then be presented with a search box for the "Family Law Cases" database and an opportunity to limit the jurisdiction to North Carolina; however, the caveat about jurisdictional comprehensiveness in the paragraph above applies here.

C. Topic Searching on Lexis Advance

1. "Browse Topics" Link above the Search Bar

Lexis Advance provides searching by subject, or more precisely, searching for relevant cases in databases containing cases already identified by Lexis as focusing on specific areas of law. To search for North Carolina cases about spousal support, for example, begin by selecting the "Browse Topics" link just above the universal search bar on the Lexis Advance starting page. Browse the "Topic Index" and select "Family Law" from the list. A detailed menu of family law subtopics will appear. Select the link for "Marital Termination & Spousal Support." At this point, you have two options:

> First, you can select "Get topic documents" and be presented with cases Lexis Advance has already identified as relevant to the selected topic. That subset of cases may then be further searched by terms and connectors, or filtered by a number of predetermined factors such as jurisdiction, court, attorney, judge, or date.

> Second, you can select "Add this topic to the search" and the subset of "Spousal Support" cases will be included in whatever search you conduct in the main Lexis Advance universal search bar.

2. "Practice Areas and Topics" Link

An easier, but slightly less narrow or specific approach for topic searching in Lexis Advance for case law is to select the "Practice Areas and Topics" link just below the universal search bar on the main page. This selection presents you with the top level Topic Index of over 40 Topics from which to choose. Choosing one or more of these Topics will add a database of pre identified cases relating to those topics to what is searched from the universal search bar. See Figure 7-5 to view the Lexis Advance "Practice Areas and Topics" page.

Figure 7-5. The Lexis Advance "Practice Areas and Topics" Page

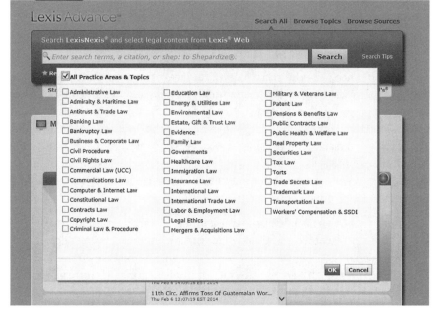

3. Working from a Retrieved Case on the Screen

Another way of accessing the "Topic Index" to find relevant cases is to apply the "one good case" method. While examining the full text of a relevant case, identify the relevant headnotes from the beginning of the case and select the subtopics listed in the headnote(s). This is similar to selecting the Topic and Key Numbers from headnotes in relevant cases while using WestlawNext. See Figure 7-6 to view an example of subtopics in headnotes from a case in Lexis Advance.

Figure 7-6. The Lexis Advance Subtopics in Case Headnotes

HN2 One of the elements of an attempt to commit a crime is that defendant have the intent to commit the substantive offense. Shepardize - Narrow by this Headnote

Criminal Law & Procedure > ... > Crimes Against Persons > Robbery > General Overview
Criminal Law & Procedure > ... > Robbery > Armed Robbery > General Overview
Criminal Law & Procedure > ... > Robbery > Armed Robbery > Elements
Criminal Law & Procedure > ... > Inchoate Crimes > Attempt > General Overview
Criminal Law & Procedure > Criminal Offenses > Weapons Offenses > General Overview
Criminal Law & Procedure > ... > Weapons Offenses > Use of Weapons > General Overview

HN3 An attempted robbery with a dangerous weapon occurs when a person, with the specific intent to unlawfully deprive another of personal property by endangering or threatening his life with a dangerous weapon, does some overt act calculated to bring about this result. Shepardize - Narrow by this Headnote

Criminal Law & Procedure > Preliminary Proceedings > Pretrial Motions & Procedures > Dismissal

HN4 The State ordinarily is not bound by the adverse testimony of its witnesses but may offer other contradicting evidence. However, when the State's case is made to rest entirely on testimony favorable to the defendant and there is no evidence contra which does more than support a possibility or raise a conjecture, demurrer thereto should be sustained. Shepardize - Narrow by this Headnote

Source: Copyright 2014 LexisNexis, a division of Reed Elsevier Inc. All rights reserved. Used with the permission of Lexis.

D. Topic Searching in Bloomberg Law

The easiest way to access topic searching in Bloomberg Law is to select the "Practice Centers" tab at the top of the main Bloomberg Law page. Bloomberg currently provides 10 practice centers, including Antitrust, Banking & Finance, Bankruptcy, Corporate/Mergers & Acquisitions, Employee Benefits, Health, Intellectual Property, Labor & Employment, Securities, and Tax. Within each center, using the link to "Opinions and dockets," the researcher has a number of ways to browse and search a subset of cases which Bloomberg has already identified as topic-relevant. See Figure 7-7 to view the "Health Practice Center" page from Bloomberg Law.

Figure 7-7. The Health Practice Center Page in Bloomberg Law

Source: Copyright 2014 The Bureau of National Affairs, Inc. All rights reserved. Used with the permission of the Bureau of National Affairs.

Chapter 8

Researching Administrative Rules and Decisions

Administrative agencies are granted power by state and federal governments that mimic the powers of all three branches of government. Agencies have quasi-legislative power, such as rule-drafting to interpret and implement legislative and executive mandates. They also have quasi-executive power, including issuing licenses, investigating whether rules are being followed, and enforcing rules. Finally, agencies can have quasi-judicial power, such as decision-making when citizens object to the rules or implementation of the rules.

But the apparently broad expanse of authority exercised by agencies is actually narrowly tailored to accomplish specific tasks. For example, every administrative rule must be authorized by other primary law, usually statutory law. An administrative rule is invalid if it exceeds the authority granting the agency power to create the rule. Administrative authority usually comes from the legislature, and these legislative acts granting authority are commonly called *enabling acts*.

Agencies create administrative law, which is composed of rules and decisions. Administrative law directly affects the lives of everyone in unimaginably detailed and wide-ranging ways. Examples of North Carolina administrative rules include rules detailing the handling of radioactive material in hospitals as well as rules specifying the number of hours a student manicurist must spend in and outside a classroom setting (including "supervised live model performances" to be eligible for licensure as a manicurist).[1]

Examples of federal administrative rules touching large issues as well as the minutia of citizens' lives also abound: many complex federal regulations detail procedures for homeland security, and more simple rules require that iodized

---

1. 21 N.C. Admin. Code 14K.0107 (2013).

salt containers include the statement "this salt supplies iodide, a necessary nutrient" in reasonably sized font on each package.[2]

This chapter will first discuss how to research North Carolina administrative law and then turn to a discussion of researching federal administrative law.

I. North Carolina Administrative Law

Administrative law initially developed without a uniform structure, process, or publication pattern. With few exceptions, federal and state agencies drafted their own regulations and made them available at agency offices. Public input in the process was minimal and public access was difficult. In the mid-1940s the federal government created the first federal "Administrative Procedures Act" addressing this issue at the federal level. Although the development was slower at the state level, most states followed a similar pattern, eventually adopting a version of the model state administrative procedures act. North Carolina's Administrative Procedures Act was first enacted in the 1970s and has been substantially amended several times.[3] The act defines the process through which administrative rules are created, the procedures to be followed in administrative hearings, and how the information is organized and published.

A. Rules

In North Carolina, a "rule" might mean any agency regulation, standard, or statement of general applicability implementing or interpreting enactments of the General Assembly or Congress.[4] Rules created within the scope of this authority and following the process prescribed by the Administrative Procedures Act have the full force and effect of law.

1. General Process of Creating Administrative Rules

A North Carolina agency proposing a new rule must publish the text of the proposed rule, along with a short reason or explanation for the rule, in a biweekly publication, the *North Carolina Register*. The public is invited to comment within a specified time period, usually at least 60 days. The agency may hold a public hearing to receive additional information. The agency considers the public comment and then may adopt the rule. If the adopted rule differs

---

2. 21 C.F.R. 100.155 (2012).

3. N.C. Gen. Stat. § 150B (2013).

4. N.C. Gen. Stat. § 150B-2(8a).

substantially from the originally proposed rule, the rule must be published again in the *North Carolina Register* and proceed through the same process again. Once the rule is adopted, the agency must keep the comments and other documentation from the rulemaking process and provide them to anyone inquiring. The agency files the adopted rule with the North Carolina Rules Review Commission, a statutory agency comprising 10 members appointed by the General Assembly. If the Rules Review Commission determines that the rule is within the authority delegated to the agency by the General Assembly and approves the rule, the rule is codified in the *North Carolina Administrative Code*. Each title of Code is organized by chapter, sometimes subchapters and sections. Chapters are often not used in identifying specific regulations. In the following example, 21 N.C. Admin. Code 14K.0107, 21 is the title, 14 is the chapter, K is the subchapter, and the section is .0107. There are two other types of rules with an abbreviated process: temporary rules and emergency rules. As you might expect, their lives are limited.

2. North Carolina Administrative Code

Two important publications provide information about North Carolina administrative rules: the *North Carolina Administrative Code* and the *North Carolina Register*.

First is the *North Carolina Administrative Code*, where rules from 26 agencies and over 50 licensing boards are organized by subject and currently updated. The official version of the *North Carolina Administrative Code* is published by West, a Thomson Reuters business, and is comprised of 30 titles published in a 20-volume set. The official version is updated with monthly supplements containing rule updates and an index.

The *Administrative Code* is also published on the North Carolina Office of Administrative Hearings website (http://reports.oah.state.nc.us/ncac.asp). Although not the official version, this convenient version is free and is updated weekly. It is browsable by title and searchable by title or full text. The *Administrative Code* is also available on WestlawNext (found by entering North Carolina Regulations in the universal search bar and selecting the title in the "Looking for this?" popup link), Lexis Advance (found through the "Browse Sources" link, narrowing the jurisdiction to North Carolina with the left margin's filters, and browsing the titles to the administrative code), and Bloomberg Law (found by selecting "All Legal Content" under the "Getting Started" heading, then selecting the "Jurisdiction" tab, narrowing the jurisdiction to North Carolina, and selecting "N.C. Regulatory and Administrative"). These databases appear to be updated at least every several months. WestlawNext also offers historical databases of previous North Carolina Administrative Codes since 2002.

3. North Carolina Register

The second important publication is the *North Carolina Register*, which is published at least every two weeks. Contents include the text of proposed rules; permanent rules approved by the Rules Review Commission; temporary rules entered into the *North Carolina Administrative Code*; emergency rules entered into the administrative code; executive orders of the Governor; and an index to published, contested administrative decisions issued by the Office of Administrative Hearings.

The *North Carolina Register* is published by LexisNexis and the print copy is available by subscription. The North Carolina Office of Administrative Hearings also publishes the *Register* on the Office's website (www.ncoah.com/rules/register). Coverage extends back to the first volume and issue in 1986, through a collaboration with the Kathrine R. Everett Law Library at the University of North Carolina School of Law.

All three major research services provide online databases to the *Register*. WestlawNext includes a *North Carolina Register* database (identified as North Carolina Administrative Register-Historical) with coverage beginning November, 2001. Lexis Advance includes a *North Carolina Register* database (found through the "Browse Sources" link, narrowing the jurisdiction to North Carolina, and browsing the titles to the *North Carolina Register*), with coverage beginning in January 2008. Bloomberg Law also provides a database of proposed, final, emergency, temporary, and interim rules, plus regulatory notices from North Carolina back to 2011 (found by selecting "All Legal Content" under the "Getting Started" heading, then selecting the "Jurisdiction" tab, narrowing the jurisdiction to North Carolina, and selecting "N.C. Regulatory and Administrative").

For researchers interested in current awareness of administrative rule activity, the Office of Administrative Hearings maintains an e-mail listserv for notification of the publication of the latest *Register* at its website.

B. Administrative Decisions

In addition to rulemaking authority, agencies also have quasi-judicial authority to settle disputes between aggrieved individuals and the agency. Agencies generally have one or two informal opportunities to settle disputes. An aggrieved citizen may then file a contested case with the Office of Administrative Hearings.

An administrative law judge (ALJ) who is independent of the agency will be appointed by the Office of Administrative Hearings to hear the case. The ALJ will issue a hearing decision to both the citizen and the agency. The agency will make the final agency decision but must adopt the ALJ's opinion unless it is contrary to the preponderance of the admissible evidence in the record. If a citizen chooses, she may appeal the agency decision to Superior Court.

Beginning in 1998, most administrative decisions have been published annually as a separate volume of the *North Carolina Administrative Code*. The volumes include the full text of all administrative decisions released for publication that year. Also included are the ALJ recommended decisions and all final agency decisions submitted to Office of Administrative Hearings. The decisions in each of these annual volumes are organized by month. In each volume, at the end of each month's decisions, is a list of decisions reported that month without published opinions, such as cases that were dismissed or where summary judgment was granted.

The decisions are also posted online at the Office of Administrative Hearings website (www.oah.state.nc.us/hearings/decisions). Coverage is browsable but not searchable. Depending upon the agency, coverage is intermittent and only available as far back as 2001, and only for a small number of agencies. WestlawNext includes a North Carolina Administrative Hearings database (found by entering "North Carolina Administrative Decisions" in the universal search bar and selecting this database from the popup window) with coverage back to 2000. At this writing, Lexis Advance only provides access to North Carolina administrative decisions concerning a small number of agencies. These may be found through the "Browse Sources" link, narrowing the jurisdiction to North Carolina, and browsing the titles to the specific agency's administrative decisions database. Likewise, Bloomberg Law only provides access to North Carolina administrative decisions concerning a small number of agencies. These may be found by selecting "All Legal Content" under the "Getting Started" heading, then selecting the "Jurisdiction" tab, narrowing the jurisdiction to North Carolina, and selecting "N.C. Agencies and Departments."

II. Researching North Carolina Administrative Rules

As with other areas of legal research, it is often easiest to find administrative rules using a source that does not contain the rules themselves. Finding relevant administrative rules is notoriously difficult for several reasons. Codifications of administrative rules are typically not well indexed. Additionally, the complex, detailed, and precise nature of the terminology involved makes the selection of search terms difficult, whether searching a print index or selecting search terms to use in a full text, keyword search.

A. Starting with a Citation to a Rule from a Secondary Source

Starting research with a secondary source is an excellent method of finding citations to administrative rules. You might begin with a law review article or a North Carolina treatise addressing a relevant topic of North Carolina law. Even if the secondary source does not provide a citation to the relevant administrative rules, the discussion might provide citations to relevant statutory law. In turn, this might provide administrative rule citations in the statutory annotations. Finally, even if the secondary sources do not provide citations to rules or related statutes, the discussion in the secondary source itself should provide clues about relevant search terms to use in a more direct keyword search, if that becomes necessary.

B. Starting with a Citation from an Authorizing or Enabling Statute

Another excellent starting point is one of the annotated codes of statutory law in North Carolina, *General Statutes of North Carolina Annotated* or *West's North Carolina General Statutes Annotated*. Because regulations must be authorized by statutory law, the enabling act providing that authority would likely cite the related administrative rules.

Alternatively, if you already have citations to the statutory law, you can approach the *Administrative Code* and use the "Table of Authority." This table is currently found in volume 20A of the *Administrative Code* and lists all of the North Carolina General Statutes, federal statutes, federal regulations, and non-statutory authority for specific rules in the North Carolina Administrative Code. This is an excellent approach to the rules when the authority for the rules is already known.

C. Browsing Titles in Print or Online

Browsing the administrative code titles is akin to the title or outline approach to searching statutory codes as discussed in Chapter 5. It is most effective when you are more familiar with the issue being researched and preferably have used the administrative code to research this issue recently. One danger in this approach is missing relevant material that is hidden in another title whose name might not suggest its relevance to the subject being researched.

In addition to the ability to browse the administrative code titles in print, the code is also browsable from the North Carolina Office of Administrative Hearings website, as well as from WestlawNext, Lexis Advance, and Bloomberg Law.

D. Searching the Index in Print

The annually published *North Carolina Administrative Code* includes an index volume as part of the set. Searching this index might be a useful approach if you are familiar with the terminology of the issue being researched. The cumulative supplements include an updated index incorporating the new regulations added to the code since the main annual index was last published.

Neither WestlawNext, Lexis Advance, or Bloomberg Law provide the index to the *North Carolina Administrative Code* online. The Office of Administrative Hearings also does not provide the index online.

E. Searching the Administrative Code Online in Full Text or by Field or Segment

Lastly, on WestlawNext or Lexis Advance you might search the full text of the administrative code or selected fields or segments of the code using keywords. Although the WestlawNext and Lexis Advance search engines have some capability to anticipate and search for additional relevant terms beyond the ones you enter, your search is most likely to succeed when you know the precise language used in the text you want to retrieve. While Bloomberg provides full text terms and connector searching, it does not currently support natural language or field or segment searching of the code.

F. Using the *North Carolina Register* to Update

Several options exist to assist with updating the rules found in the annually published *North Carolina Administrative Code*. First, check the citation in the cumulative supplement. Checking the index in the cumulative supplement might also catch any related but non-connected new rules. Next, check each *North Carolina Register* issued since the date of the most recent cumulative supplement for any newly approved rules, new temporary rules, or new emergency rules.

III. Researching North Carolina Administrative Decisions

Each of the "Administrative Decisions" volumes of the *North Carolina Administrative Code* includes an index. Additionally, new decisions are included in the cumulative supplements throughout the year. The decisions reported in each of those supplements are also indexed. Finally, each *North Carolina Register* includes decisions from the previous weeks and should be browsed.

Administrative decisions may also be researched online. The decisions are free and browsable (although not searchable) by agency and by year at the Office of Administrative Hearings website, although the coverage is far from comprehensive. WestlawNext maintains a searchable database of North Carolina agency decisions. Lexis Advance and Bloomberg Law maintain several databases of a small number of agency decisions.

IV. North Carolina Attorney General Opinions

The North Carolina Attorney General is statutorily required to issue opinions on questions of law submitted by the General Assembly, the Governor, Auditor, Treasurer or other state officers.[5] While these opinions are not law, they represent the state's interpretation of the law applied to a specific question and are very persuasive.[6]

The most convenient and least expensive method of researching Attorney General Opinions is to use the North Carolina Department of Justice's website (www.ncdoj.gov/About-DOJ/Legal-Services/Legal-Opinions.aspx) to search or browse the opinions. The collection contains opinions issued since 1977. Researchers may also contact the office directly for copies of opinions that are not available online.

The opinions are also available with similar coverage on WestlawNext and can be found by entering "North Carolina Attorney General Opinions" in the universal search bar. The Attorney General Opinions database is found on Lexis Advance by selecting "Browse Sources" and then narrowing to North Carolina. Bloomberg Law's coverage of North Carolina Attorney General Opin-

---

5. N.C. Gen. Stat. § 114-2(5).

6. See the North Carolina case, *Lawrence v. Shaw*, stating that Attorney General Opinions are advisory only. *Lawrence v. Shaw*, 210 N.C. 352, 361, 186 S.E. 504, 509 (1936), *rev'd on other grounds*, 300 U.S. 245, 57 S. Ct. 443, 81 L. Ed. 623 (1937).

ions begins with December 1955; this database can be found by selecting "All Legal Content" under the "Getting Started" heading, then selecting the "Jurisdiction" tab, narrowing the jurisdiction to North Carolina, and selecting "N.C. Agencies and Departments."

Various law libraries around the state have paper copies of opinions with coverage back to 1901 and earlier. At various periods through history, the opinions have been issued in the *Attorney General Reports*. The paper collections have various indexing through the years but may be difficult to research. For opinions since 1977, online sources will usually provide better access for researchers, especially for those researchers without a citation.

V. Federal Administrative Law

Federal administrative law is created and operates in much the same manner as North Carolina administrative law. The first federal code of administrative law was published in 1938. The first federal Administrative Procedures Act was enacted in 1946 for the purpose of requiring agencies to keep the public informed of agency organization, procedures, and regulations. The act also provided a method for public participation in the rulemaking process, standardized the rulemaking process, and confirmed the idea of judicial review of administrative decisions.

Unlike North Carolina administrative "rules," at the federal level the administrative rules are referred to as administrative "regulations." Federal administrative regulations have the full force and effect of law when created within the parameters of the Administrative Procedures Act.[7]

A. Administrative Regulations

Federal regulations are created in a similar manner as North Carolina rules. Upon receiving authority to draft rules governing a specific issue, an agency will investigate and use its expertise to propose regulations. The proposed regulations are published in the *Federal Register*. The public has a specific period of time in which to respond. The agency may hold one or more public hearings about the proposed regulations. Regulations.gov is a website where the public may conveniently find, view, and comment on proposed federal regulations. The agency will consider the public feedback and then issue final regulations,

---

7. *Atchison, T. & S.F. Ry. Co. v. Scarlett*, 300 U.S. 471, 57 S. Ct. 541 (1937).

which also must be published in the *Federal Register*. Thereafter, the final regulations will be codified in the *Code of Federal Regulations*.

1. *Code of Federal Regulations*

The *Code of Federal Regulations* (CFR) is similar to the *North Carolina Administrative Code*. CFR is a compilation of all the federal administrative regulations currently in effect. It is arranged by agency, which is a rough arrangement by subject. The CFR contains 50 titles and the structure is similar to federal statutory law in the United States Code. While some of the titles correspond, like title 26 addressing the Internal Revenue Service, more often than not the correlation does not exist. As discussed later, however, that does not keep the United States Code from being a good source for finding relevant regulations. Each title of CFR is organized by chapter, part, and section. Chapters are often not used in identifying specific regulations. For the following example, 20 CFR 416.906, 20 is the title, 416 is the part, and the section is .906. Often, when speaking of the section, the part is included without being stated. A lawyer might say "section 416.906."

The CFR is published annually in paperback form by the Government Printing Office. Rather than publishing the entire set at one time, GPO publishes one quarter of it every three months so that the entire set is republished over the course of a year. The paper covers of the individual volumes change color each year, which makes identifying updated volumes much easier. Often, the volumes are months late being updated and distributed, and many volumes straggle from the publisher at different times, even volumes addressing parts of the same title.

In addition to printing the CFR, the Government Printing Office also posts CFR at the Federal Digital System website (www.gpo.gov/fdsys).[8] At this writing, the text of the annual CFR edition at the website is generally no more current than the print copy. GPO also produces the "Electronic Code of Federal Regulations" (e-CFR), which is an authentic but unofficial editorial compilation of CFR incorporating the latest amendments as published in the *Federal Register*. e-CFR is a project of GPO and the National Archives and Records Administration's Office of the Federal Register. It is typically updated and current within several days of any changes published in the *Federal Register* affecting currently codified regulations. Because e-CFR is not designated as official, it should not be solely relied upon for legal purposes.

---

8. Prior to 2010, the GPO website that hosted CFR was GPO Access at www.gpoaccess.gov/cfr/index.html.

WestlawNext, Lexis Advance, and Bloomberg Law also provide a fee-based CFR database that, like GPO's e-CFR, is updated within days of changes published in the *Federal Register*. HeinOnline is an excellent comprehensive source for historical versions of the CFR.

2. *Federal Register*

The *Federal Register* serves the same purpose as the *North Carolina Register*. It is published every business day, however, rather than biweekly. The *Federal Register* serves as the official publication of proposed and final regulations, as well as notices from federal agencies and some Presidential documents such as executive orders.

The *Federal Register* often contains an agency's reasoning behind the regulatory scheme or changes in a Notice of Proposed Rulemaking. In the final version of the rules, explanations of changes and responses to comments made by the public or interested organizations and business are often included. This makes the *Federal Register* a rich source for interpreting the meaning of the rules and predicting the choices and arguments an agency is likely to make when enforcing the rules.

The best access to the *Federal Register* is provided online by the publisher, GPO, at the FDsys website (www.gpo.gov/fdsys) where it is updated every day by 6:00 a.m. It is freely available and both browsable and searchable. WestlawNext, Lexis Advance, and Bloomberg Law also provide online access through currently updated databases that are fee-based. Again, HeinOnline is an excellent comprehensive source for historical versions of the *Federal Register*.

3. Researching Federal Administrative Regulations

Researching a legal subject in the print version of CFR is challenging. As with North Carolina rules, researching federal regulations is best begun in secondary sources. Reading more about a legal issue in secondary sources might actually produce citations to relevant regulations. Alternatively, citations to relevant United States Code sections might be revealed in secondary source material that would be helpful in the research process. Lastly, the understanding and terminology gained from the secondary source will only improve the researcher's ability to conduct effective full text, keyword searches in CFR, if necessary.

Because the United States Code is generally easier to search than CFR, the next best starting point for legal subject searching would be the *United States Code Service* or the *United States Code Annotated*. These annotated codes should provide citations to relevant regulations. Historically, the *United States Code Service* has done a superior job connecting the statutes to the regulations.

Additional options for searching for relevant regulations include browsing the CFR titles and chapters, or using the single-volume index found in the last volume of the CFR set. Each presents challenges. The title names are not always helpful in identifying the scope of regulations they contain. The index only indexes regulations down to the "part" level rather than the "section" level and is notoriously not very detailed. When using the index, you must locate the part and then browse the list of sections in the specific volume to find the most relevant sections.

Online options for researching federal regulations abound, and tend to be more convenient, if not more productive. The online version of CFR from GPO is browsable and searchable by keyword, citation, or title. Because it's directly posted by GPO and is freely available at the Federal Digital System, use of this database is highly recommended. GPO's e-CFR is also useful, especially due to its current updating.

WestlawNexts's, Lexis Advance's, and Bloomberg Law's versions of CFR are also currently updated and provide keyword- and title-browsable access. West-lawNext provides a browsable index hyperlinked into relevant portions of the CFR. This is also an excellent online option for researching regulations.

B. Updating Administrative Regulations

1. Online

The best way to update a federal regulation is to use e-CFR, the Federal Digital System (FDsys), as the starting point. This resource should provide the date through which the most recent changes to regulations were last incorporated into the text. Next, approach the *Federal Register* issues at FDsys that have been published since the most recent incorporation date from e-CFR. Examine the "CFR Sections Affected" chart in the most recent issue of the *Federal Register* to make sure your section has not been amended. A similar method should be used if updating the CFR database from WestlawNext, Lexis Advance, or Bloomberg Law. Very little updating is necessary with the e-CFR, West-lawNext, Lexis Advance, or Bloomberg Law databases.

To update the official annual edition of the CFR from the Federal Digital System (FDsys) you must use the "List of Sections Affected" database which should cover the period from the annual edition publication date until the current date. This process is very similar to the process for updating the print version of CFR. Just as with print, any gap in time between the coverage of the "List of Sections Affected" database and the current date must be covered using the daily Federal Registers. This process might be more intuitive after reviewing the following explanation of updating CFR in print.

2. Print

Updating the print version of CFR is more cumbersome. This same cumbersome process must also be followed when updating the official annual CFR database at FDsys, since it is no more current than the print version. Regardless of the source of the annual edition (print or FDsys), and assuming the title you are updating is more than one month past publication, there is a two-step process for updating a paper regulation. The updating process is similar to checking pocket parts, except that you will use a separate publication called the *List of Sections Affected* (LSA) and the back page of the *Federal Register*.

a. List of Sections Affected *Monthly Pamphlet*

First, find the most recent pamphlet (or database on FDsys) known as *List of Sections Affected* (LSA). LSA is a monthly publication that lists all sections of CFR that have been affected by recent rulemaking activity. Information in LSA should be current back to the publication date of your paper CFR volume; however, you should cautiously confirm the dates of coverage for the LSA publication or database to ensure coverage.

If there is no reference to a section containing your regulation in LSA, there have been no changes to your regulation between the date the CFR Title was last published and the date of the LSA. If however, there has been a change, this table will list the *Federal Register* page number for each new agency action that has affected your specific section.

b. Federal Register *"CFR Parts Affected"* Table

The second step involves examining a table in the back of the *Federal Register*. The table is called the "CFR Parts Affected for [the current month]." Search the table for reference to your CFR section. Search this table in each *Federal Register* volume published on the last day of each month since the most recently published, monthly LSA.

When you reach the current month, search this same table in the most recent *Federal Register* issue. The chart in the back of the *Federal Register* is always cumulative for the entire month. If you use the free online issues of *Federal Register* at the FDsys website, which are updated each morning by 6:00 a.m., this process will update your regulation to same-day currency. The paper *Federal Register* will probably be a week or two old due to mailing and processing.

3. Updating with Citators

In addition to updating the regulations themselves, a researcher should also use citators such as Shepard's on Lexis Advance or KeyCite on WestlawNext to find all related information citing a specific regulation being researched.

C. Administrative Decisions

As with North Carolina agencies, federal agencies issue a number of types and levels of decisions. Federal administrative decisions are much more variable and widely dispersed. Agency decisions were traditionally published in individual print reporters. For example, *Federal Trade Commission Decisions* is a reporter for the decisions of the Federal Trade Commission. A number of agency decisions were also published in private publications by publishers such as Commerce Clearing House (CCH) and Bureau of National Affairs (BNA). For more information about official and unofficial reporters of agency decisions, see a selected list of agency reporters, see Table 1.2 (T1.2) of the *Bluebook*, "Federal Administrative and Executive Materials."[9]

More recent federal agency decisions are being published directly at the agency websites. For example, the Federal Trade Commission now provides access to commission decisions back to 1969. Agency websites are independent and also vary widely in terms of organization and information provided. These websites can easily be found online using a search engine such as Google. Alternatively, you may use a collection of links to "Administrative Decisions and Other Actions" posted by the University of Virginia Library (http:// guides.lib.virginia.edu/administrative_decisions). This site might be particularly useful if you do not initially know which agency might publish the decisions you need or you are uncertain of the level of decision you need from a large agency. Recent agency decisions are also selectively available in fee-based databases at WestlawNext, Lexis Advance, and Bloomberg Law.

Once all administrative remedies have been exhausted, dissatisfied parties may have the opportunity to appeal an administrative decision to federal court. Once the issues from a specific administrative decision enter the federal court system, researching the issues becomes case law research, which is addressed in Chapter 7.

---

9. See the *Bluebook*, table T1.2, at 218.

VI. Researching U.S. Attorney General Opinions

The Office of the United States Attorney General was created by the Judiciary Act of 1789. The Attorney General is the head of the Justice Department (created in 1870) and serves as the chief law enforcement officer of the federal government. Among other duties, the U.S. Attorney General gives advice and issues opinions upon request to the President and the heads of the executive departments of the federal government. The Attorney General has delegated to the U.S. Department of Justice Office of Legal Counsel the duties of providing legal advice to the President and executive branch agencies. These duties include the drafting of the formal opinions of the Attorney General.

Selected opinions back to 1992 may be found for free at the Office of Legal Counsel website (www.usdoj.gov/olc/opinions.htm). They are browsable by year. Selected opinions are also available on WestlawNext, Lexis Advance, and Bloomberg Law. Just as with opinions of the North Carolina Attorney General, opinions of the U.S. Attorney General are only persuasive as an educated interpretation of federal law applied to specific facts.[10] The opinions are not law.

---

10. For a discussion of how Attorney General Opinions are researched, drafted, and published, see the "Memorandum for Attorneys of the Office, RE: Best Practices for OLC Legal Advice and Written Opinions" at http://www.justice.gov/olc/preparation-opinions.html.

Chapter 9

Updating Research

I. Introduction

A. Reasons for Updating

Law is a living, growing body of knowledge that is constantly changing. In the practice of law, therefore, access to the most current information is critically important for several reasons. Most importantly, a lawyer must know if the authority she is relying on is still "good law." For a case, the determination of good law means whether that particular case was reversed on appeal to a higher court or overruled by a subsequently decided case in the same jurisdiction. For a statute or administrative rule, the determination of good law means that it has not been amended, appealed, or superseded by subsequent legislation or overruled by a case.

Updating research has several other important purposes. While law found online or in print through a comprehensive, modern research process will likely still be good law, the law changes quickly and updating your research is still critically important. Law is being created, decided, and applied on a daily basis. Even if your authority has not been directly affected, subsequently decided cases might strengthen or weaken its application in certain situations. Beyond your case being good law, you need to know how your case has been treated by subsequent sources.

A third reason to update your authority is to find cases similar to yours for research purposes. This can be an especially useful research tool if, for example, you have one or only a few cases and are having difficulty identifying additional cases. The process of updating usually identifies any related authorities that have been issued after your case was decided.

Fourth, updating ensures you have found the most current information from each source. Some online databases are currently updated by the organization supporting the database. For some print sources, initial updating may involve searching books, pocket parts, and pamphlets in combination. Regardless of the source, be sure to observe how current the information is that you are using by looking at scope notes for databases and date references or copyright dates for print information. Then after retrieving the most current information from each source throughout your research process, you should also use a *citator* to complete the updating process. For example, if you are using a citator to update a case, the citator will list every other authority that includes at least a mere reference to your case. To be thorough, you must examine each of the documents listed in the citator as citing your case to determine (1) whether your case is still good law, (2) how your case has been treated by subsequent decisions, and (3) what other cases or statutes are available that are related to this issue.

B. Citators

Shepard's Citations Service was the preeminent name in citators for over 100 years. Although a trademarked name, its ubiquitous existence as the only citator for generations of attorneys and researchers across the country led to the creation of the term "Shepardizing" to describe the act of updating the law with a citator.

In North Carolina, as in the rest of the United States, online citators are the preferred method of updating because they are easy to use and kept very current.[1] Shepard's Citations Service is available on Lexis Advance. In addition, Westlaw developed a competing online product in the 1990s known as KeyCite, which is available on WestlawNext. Bloomberg Law has also developed a citator called BCite. Each of these important citators will be discussed below in turn, in the context of updating case law. The chapter ends with a brief discussion of how to use Shepard's and KeyCite to update a statute.

---

1. Online citators are typically updated with information within about 24–48 hours of its creation. Because of their superiority as research tools, this chapter will focus on the use of online citators. Note that Shepard's remains available as a print publication. Researchers in North Carolina may use *Shepard's North Carolina Citations,* which lists authorities citing each case published in *North Carolina Reports, North Carolina Court of Appeals Reports,* and *West's South Eastern Reporter.* Another Shepard's set, *Shepard's South Eastern Reporter Citations,* provides lists of cases citing each case published in the *South Eastern Reporter.* Although not complex, the use of Shepard's in print is cumbersome and the information is limited in time by the printing and distribution process. The most current information available in print might still be two to four weeks old. If you are ever faced with using Shepard's in print, consult the detailed instructions included in the "Guide to Shepard's" section in the softbound supplements.

Shepard's, KeyCite, and BCite share some common features. First, important terminology is similar. The authority being updated, in this discussion a case, is called the *cited source*. All of the citations listed by the citator are documents that cite your case, the cited source. All of the documents listed in the citator as citing your case are called *citing sources* or *citing references*. The process of updating involves examining each of the citing sources or citing references to see how they treat your case. Shepard's, KeyCite, and BCite provide editorial enhancements for some of the citing sources or references suggesting how they treat your case, the cited source. While these enhancements may be relied upon to prioritize research, these editorial notes about treatment should never be solely relied upon in the practice of law or for other important research projects. Each relevant citing source or citing reference should be examined. Fortunately, all three systems can help winnow the list of citing references by jurisdiction and Shepard's and KeyCite can do so by point of law in the cited case.

Color-coded symbols suggest how the citing source or reference treats the cited source. Just as headnotes should not be solely relied upon to explain how legal issues are dealt with in a case without reading the text of that case, the color-coded symbols should not be relied upon to indicate how a citing source treats a cited source. The assignment of the symbols is dependent upon an editor's interpretation of the issues and outcome in each case. While there are editorial safeguards in place to prevent error, human error or legitimate difference of opinion is always possible. Additionally, since there are often multiple legal issues in cases, a symbol assigned to a case might only reference a part of the case not relevant to your research. The symbols should only be used to prioritize the order in which the citing references are examined. The color-coded symbols for each service are described in Tables 9-1, 9-3, and 9-4 later in the chapter.

II. Updating Cases Using Shepard's on Lexis Advance

A. Accessing Shepard's

There are several ways to Shepardize a case.

1. Shepardizing a Case Displayed on the Screen

Once a case is retrieved and displayed on the screen, select the "Shepardize" button or click the signal near the case name. Shepard's will then produce a citation report for that case.

2. Shepardizing a Case Using the Citation

When you already have a case citation, you might simply need to view the Shepard's citations report without viewing the text of the case in Lexis Advance first. You may Shepardize a case using a citation. Simply type the citation into the universal search bar and select the Shepard's button (located within the red search box) instead of the grey Search button.

B. The Shepard's Display

The Shepard's display defaults to the list view of the appellate history portion of the Shepard's report. This tab provides the subsequent history of your case. To view this information in an interactive visual format, click the "Map" button. With complex litigation, the visual presentation can answer many questions and make the flow of litigation in the case more understandable. The case names in the chart are linked to the full text of the decisions, just as they would be in a citation list.

To view all of the cases that cite your case, click on the "Citing Decisions" tab. This tab lists every case decision in the Lexis Advance system that cites your case. By default, the cases are listed by jurisdiction with the newest cases from each court first. To change the order, simply click on the category along the top of the list. These include analysis, discussion (how much the citing case discusses your case), court, and date. You can also change the order by using the "Sort by" drop-down menu.

Clicking the "Analysis" link will bring cases with negative analysis to the top. Lexis Advance editors label each case with an analysis label to indicate how the citing case treats your case. These include negative labels such as "criticized" or "distinguished," positive labels such as "followed," and neutral labels such as "explained," "harmonized," or cited in an concurring or dissenting opinion. In addition, each analysis is categorized and labeled with a corresponding colored square that corresponds to the symbols assigned to cases: warning (red), questioned (orange), caution (yellow), positive (green), and neutral or unknown (blue). See Figure 9-1 for an example of the "Citing Decisions" tab of a Shepard's report on Lexis Advance for a North Carolina Court of Appeals decision, *Cody v. Snider Lumber Co.*, 96 N.C. App. 293, 385 S.E.2d 515 (1989).

Figure 9-1. Shepard's Citing Decisions Tab

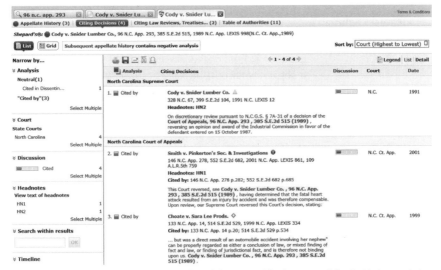

Source: Copyright 2014 LexisNexis, a division of Reed Elsevier Inc. All rights reserved. Used with the permission of Lexis.

The tab for "Citing Law Reviews, Treatises, Annotated Statutes, Court Documents, Restatements, and other Secondary Sources" (usually displayed as "Citing Law Reviews, Treatises …") provides a list of all secondary source documents on Lexis Advance that cite your case.

The "Table of Authorities" tab lists all of the cases cited within your case along with an analysis status and a status symbol for those cases. Although not a substitute for a thorough analysis of these cases, this list can give a quick indication of the overall status of the authority on which your case relies.

C. The Meaning and Use of the Citator Symbols

Shepard's employs a number of symbols to express the editors' judgment about the value of a cited case so that you may quickly make a reasonable assessment of whether your case is still good law. In addition, the editors assess the value of each case citing your case and assign symbols. These symbols should be used cautiously, and you should read the text of the cases to make your own assessment. The real value in using the symbols is to assist in prioritizing the order in which you read the citing references. Table 9-1 lists and defines the Shepard's symbols.

Table 9-1. Symbols for Updating Cases with Shepard's

Shepard's Symbol	Definition
Red "Stop" Sign	Warning, the editors have identified strong negative treatment for at least one legal issue in this case. At least part of the case may possibly have been overruled or reversed.
Orange "Q"	The editors found at least one citing source that questions one of the legal issues in the case, which might affect its precedential value.
Yellow Triangle	The handling of at least one legal issue in your case has been criticized by or distinguished by another case.
Blue "I"	One or more cases cite your case without giving your case any treatment. For example, a case may simply cite your case.
Blue "A"	The editors found at least one case citing your case that addresses your case, but that treatment is neutral. For example, the citing case may explain your case without stating a positive or negative interpretation.
Green "+" Sign	There is only positive treatment for your case, such as "affirmed" or "follow by."

The symbols may appear in several places within the report. The most important symbol is the one at the top of the screen next to the name of your case. Scroll over the symbol for a quick reminder of the symbol's meaning. Alternatively, Shepard's provides a quick signal legend at the top right of the screen. Citing cases or references may also have symbols beside them, indicating the strength of each of those cases. While that could be important if a case treating your case negatively was later reversed or overruled, generally you are mostly interested in the symbol applied to your case at the top of the screen. The significance of these two different placements of the symbols should not be confused.

D. Narrowing the Citing Documents

For cases that have been frequently cited and display a lengthy citation report, it may be useful to limit the type of information included in the report. The more frequently cited your case, however, the more critically important these filters become. The extreme example is *Roe v. Wade*, 410 U.S. 113 (1973). With over 16,000 documents on Lexis citing *Roe v. Wade*, the only reasonable way of beginning to analyze the citing references is to filter the citing cases.

Shepard's offers several ways to narrow the results: analysis, court, discussion, headnotes, keyword, and timeline. These categories appear down the left side of the report. See Figure 9-1 for an example. This feature is responsive, so it will show only the options that exist for your case.

Narrowing by analysis allows you to view cases that treat your case in a particular way. In the analysis filter, the more negative options appear at the top (assuming your case has received any negative treatment). This is a handy way to jump to cases that treat your cases in a negative manner; remember to read these cases themselves rather than relying exclusively on the judgment of the editors. Focusing on positive treatment allows you to limit the report to cases that would strengthen reliance on your case. These cases might also contain more useful fact comparisons or more detailed analysis than your cited case.

The court section in the menu of filters allows you to narrow your results to cases in a particular jurisdiction. This is extremely helpful especially when the time you can spend analyzing the report is limited or when your cases has been cited extensively. Note that you can select multiple courts at once.

The discussion filter allows you to review only cases that analyze or discuss your case rather than those that simply mention or cite it in passing

To narrow to cases that cite your case for a particular issue or topic, use the headnote filter. If you do not remember which headnotes are relevant, simply pause your cursor over the headnote number to be reminded of the topic.

It is also possible to search for terms within all of the documents listed on the Shepard's report. A search box is provided in the list of filters.

The timeline section allows you to narrow the results to a particular time period and displays a graph of how often your case has been cited over time. To narrow the time period, simply type the years into the two boxes and click the "OK" box.

E. Analyzing the Citing Sources' Treatment of Your Case

Although the editors provide glitzy symbols alerting you to positive and potentially negative treatment of your case, it is your ethical and moral responsibility to interpret how the citing references affect your case. The essence of updating with citators is the application of your professional judgment to the analysis given your case by the citing cases or references and to determine the affect.

Clicking on the name of a citing reference in the list links you to the relevant part of that case that cites and perhaps discusses your case. If the pinpointed information about your case seems relevant, be sure to read the entire case or other source so that the pinpointed information is understood in the larger context of the whole citing reference.

In addition to positive and negative treatment, you might discover that many cases cite your case for another point of law and are therefore not relevant to your inquiry. Also, a number of citing cases may simply cite your case without ascribing any meaning or value to it. These citing cases should be disregarded.

Several other benefits may flow from the time and effort spent updating cases. For example, one of the cases citing your case may actually be more appropriate factually or legally to support your claim or defense. One of the citing cases might also raise addition relevant issues you had yet to consider. Because of these research benefits, you would be wise to update cases throughout the research process rather than waiting until the end of the process.

III. Updating Cases Using KeyCite on WestlawNext

A. Accessing KeyCite

When a case (or other document) is displayed on WestlawNext, KeyCite information is automatically provided in tabs along the top of the screen. See Figure 9-2 for an example of how the information is displayed for a North Carolina case, *Cody v. Snider Lumber Co.*, 96 N.C. App. 293, 385 S.E.2d 515 (1989). The KeyCite status symbol is prominently displayed next to the case name. The tabs along the top of the case text link to various parts of the KeyCite report.

B. The KeyCite Display

The "History" tab provides the direct history, both prior and subsequent, of your case. This list includes whether your case reversed or remanded a lower court's ruling, or whether your case was appealed and its disposition. This information is provided in both a list and graphical form. When the cited case was part of complex litigation, the graphical presentation can answer questions and help you understand the flow of litigation in the case. The case names in the chart are linked to the full text of the decisions, just as they are in the list.

The Negative Treatment tab presents any negative direct history followed by citing cases that treat your case negatively. This list includes cases that overrule, criticize, distinguish, modify or call into doubt the cited case. The cases are organized by treatment (with the most negative listed first) and then by

Figure 9-2. KeyCite Tabs

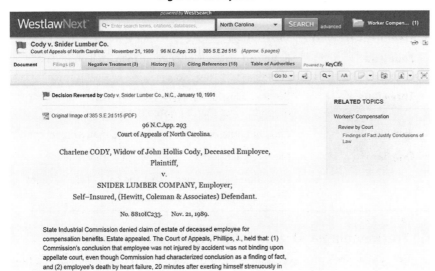

Source: Reprinted with permission of Thomson-Reuters.

jurisdiction in reverse chronological order. You cannot resort or filter the order of the cases with this tab. To use that functionality, click over to the "Citing References" tab.

The "Citing References" tab lists all of the documents that cite your case. The default order presented starts with cases that have the most discussion of your case. Within this order, negative cases are always listed first. This order can be changed to sort by date, using the "Sort By" link at the top of the page. KeyCite uses depth of treatment bars to denote the extent to which citing references analyze your case. Citing cases examining your case in the greatest depth are presented first and those only mentioning your case insignificantly are at the bottom of the list. See Table 9-2 for an explanation of the symbols used.

The "Table of Authorities" tab lists all of the cases that are cited by your case, along with status flags for those cases, giving you a quick indication of the overall status of the authority on which your case relies. Remember that skimming this list is not a substitute for reading cases yourself.

Table 9-2. KeyCite Depth of Treatment Symbols

Treatment Symbols	Description
Four Bars	Examined in depth, often more than a full printed page of text
Three Bars	Discussed less extensively, typically more than a paragraph but less than a printed page
Two Bars	Cited but little discussion, usually less than a paragraph
One Bar	Mentioned insignificantly, often in a string citation
" "	Quotation marks suggest that the citing case includes direct quotation from your case

C. The Meaning and Use of the KeyCite Status Flags

Just as Shepard's on Lexis assigns symbols such as a red stop sign or a yellow triangle to cases to denote how that case has been treated by subsequent cases, KeyCite uses flags for the same purpose. Anytime a case is viewed on West-lawNext, it may have a KeyCite status flag next to the title of the case. The status flag is a quick reference symbol indicating the editors' opinion about whether the case is still "good law." Although not to be relied upon as authoritative, this quick indication of the strength of a case can be useful for prioritizing your research and delving into your own inquiry about the strength of the case. Note this symbol when researching cases as a starting point to determine the validity of the case. A list of the KeyCite symbols and a brief description can be found in Table 9-3.

Table 9-3. KeyCite Status Flags

KeyCite Flag	Description
Red Flag	Warning, the editors discovered strong negative treatment, such as the case being reversed on appeal or overturned by another case, and determined it is no longer "good law" for at least one legal point.
Yellow Flag	The editors found some negative treatment but the case has not been reversed or overturned.

D. Limiting the Search Results

When a case has been cited by many other cases, it may not be realistic to attempt to review each case. Recall from the discussion of Shepard's, for example, that *Roe v. Wade* has been cited by an unmanageable amount of documents. There are over 22,000 documents on WestlawNext. Due to time constraints, a best practice would be to use the citator service to assist in prioritizing the order of importance in which citing cases are reviewed. Certainly those cases suggesting negative treatment should be reviewed first. KeyCite offers ways of limiting the citations report to information that is most relevant to your research.

When viewing the "Citing References" tab, which lists all documents on WestlawNext that cite your case, you can view the options for filtering the list in the left margin. This list will be different depending on the characteristics of the citing documents. For example, if no cases cite your document, that filter will not appear in the left margin. Further, if only North Carolina cases cite your authority, only that state will be listed under the "Jurisdiction" filter.

Potential filters include for cases include keyword, jurisdiction, date, depth of treatment, headnote, treatment status, and reported status. To use more than one filter, click on "Select Multiple Filters."

The citing cases' jurisdiction filter is most useful, for example, when researching a federal case where you might only be interested in citing cases from the federal Court of Appeals for the Fourth Circuit or federal cases from North Carolina.

Another useful limitation of the citation report involves the headnotes from your case. KeyCite allows you to limit the citation list to only those cases addressing the legal issue discussed in one of the headnotes from your case.

As discussed above, KeyCite analyzes the depth of treatment each citing case provides your case. The depth of treatment limitation is useful when you only wish to view citing cases discussing your case in greatest depth, for example.

Cases can also be filtered by their publication status. This can be useful if you are researching in a jurisdiction that only permits citation to reported or published cases.

The various document types of the citing references may also be limited. You would use the limitation when only interested in citations from a state's highest court, or only from secondary sources in general or particular secondary sources, or only from specific types of court documents.

A specific date or time frame may also be used as a limit.

Figure 9-3. KeyCite Filters

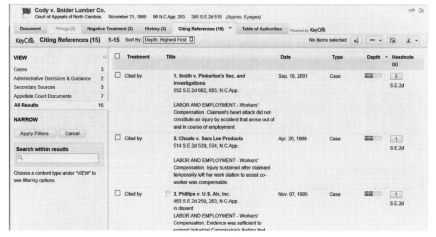

Source: Reprinted with permission of Thomson-Reuters.

If you work with just one filter at a time, KeyCite will automatically apply the filter as you click on the box (e.g., clicking on a particular headnote or depth of treatment). Often you will work with multiple filters. After selecting the desired limitations, select the "Apply Filters" button to ensure that the limitations are applied to the citation list. See Figure 9-3 to view the KeyCite case filters available for *Cody v. Snider Lumber Co.*

E. Analyzing the Citing Sources' Treatment of Your Case

Again, there is no substitute for examining the cases yourself. Certainly all the cases relied upon from the citations report should be closely examined and the legal issues from each case understood within the entire context of that case and not read in isolation.

IV. Updating Cases Using BCite on Bloomberg Law

As a relative newcomer to the legal market, Bloomberg Law's BCite is the newest citator product. It was developed in the 2000s, when Bloomberg Law decided to add an editorially created citator to its product. Bloomberg's staff reviewed all of the cases on Bloomberg to create BCite.

When viewing a case on Bloomberg Law, the BCite symbol appears next to the case name to indicate the general status of the case. Details appear on the right in the BCite Analysis pane and in the tabs across the top of the document.

Your case's prior and subsequent history can be viewed by clicking the "Direct History" link or tab. The total number of cases citing your case, along with a breakdown by treatment indicator (such as positive, distinguished, or criticized) is shown in the pane to the right of the case text. See Table 9-4 for a list of the possible BCite indicators.

Table 9-4. BCite Indicators

BCite Symbols	Description
Green Plus Sign	Positive, the editors found no citing cases or found cases that follow or discuss the case with approval
Blue Checkmark	Distinguished, the editors determined that at least one case differentiated the case on the facts or the law
Yellow Triangle	Caution, the editors discovered either a case in the direct history that modified or clarified the cited case or any case that criticized the cited case's legal reasoning without directly overruling it
Orange Circle	Superseded by statute, the editors decided that at least one court has affirmatively stated that the opinion has been rendered obsolete, displaced, or superseded by a statute or regulation
Red Minus Sign	Negative, at least part of the cited case is reversed, vacated, or depublished in full or in part by a case in its direct history, at least part of the case has been overruled by any court.
Grey X	Pending, Bloomberg Law editors are reviewing the case

To view all of the cases that cite your case, click the "Case Analysis" link or tab. By default, this list is in pure chronological order, but can be changed to sort by most cited cases (called citation frequency), citing case analysis (which brings the most negative treatment to the top), or by court. BCite also offers a number of filters that can be used to limit the results: analysis, status, citation frequency, court, judge, and date. The citing case analysis allows you to see cases that have treated your case in a particular way, such as "criticized" or "distinguished." The status filter allows you to see cases with a particular status (such as negative). Note that there is not a way to limit the results by topic or subject on this tab. There is a topic filter for cases, though, on the "Citing Documents" tab.

The "Citing Documents" tab provides a list of all documents on Bloomberg Law that cite your case, including court opinions. You can filter the results by type of document and date. Once you have filtered by type of document, additional filters may be available. For example, the court opinions filter allows you to filter by the topic of the citing case.

The "Table of Authorities" tab lists the cases cited within your case and indicates how these cases were treated by your case and the general status symbol for each case, quickly suggesting the overall status of the authority on which your case relies.

V. Prioritizing Citing Sources

Regardless of the system used, the best practice is not to rely fully on a publisher's editorial judgment or opinions. When a researcher does not have time to read and examine all the cases in a citing list, however, she must use her best professional judgment in determining the best use of her time when fulfilling her ethical and moral obligation to her client or the person for whom she is researching. Consider some of the following issues when prioritizing which citing references to read within a restricted time frame.

Indications of negative treatment should be given highest priority. It is critical to know of any subsequent appeal of your case resulting in a reversal. Other citing references that the editors believe overruled, criticized, or even simply distinguished your case should be closely evaluated.

Next, limit the citing references to cases within your jurisdiction since you are mainly interested in primary, mandatory authority. This strategy is particularly true for federal cases. The strategy might be less useful when updating North Carolina cases since most of the citing references will be from North Carolina.

Also prioritize your reading and analysis by court hierarchy. While Shepard's arranges citing references in hierarchical order by highest court, KeyCite lists citing cases by depth of treatment. The KeyCite list, however, can also be limited to only the decisions from the highest court within each jurisdiction. The BCite list is presented in pure chronological order, so you should use the filters to prioritize cases in your jurisdiction.

Another limiting strategy to assist in prioritizing reading and evaluation of citing cases is to limit by date so that the most recent cases are read first.

Using headnotes to limit the citing cases is another excellent method of prioritization. If a case deals with multiple topics, you may be interested in it only for one topic. Limiting citing cases to those cases that discuss the issue in which you are interested provides only relevant results. Although BCite does allow filtering by topic, it is the general topic of the citing case—not the point of law in the cited case being discussed in the citing case. This is generally less useful.

VI. Updating Statutes

State and federal statutes may be updated using either Shepard's or KeyCite. Bloomberg Law's BCite does not cover statutes at this time. Because statutes are different from cases in the way that they are created and updated, the results from KeyCite and Shepard's when updating statutes is different from those retrieved when updating cases. Fortunately, the concept and process of updating statutes are similar to the process for updating cases.

The process of updating statutes using citators is similar to the process for cases. On Lexis Advance, click on the "View Shepard's Report" link. On WestlawNext, KeyCite tabs will be displayed across the top of the documentNext, view the listed citing sources and examine any accompanying symbols. If necessary, restrict the search. The final and most important step is to carefully examine the citing sources to determine whether and how they affect the statute. The information retrieved when updating statutes differs as follows.

A. Using KeyCite to Update Statutes

KeyCite information is integrated into each statute document. The "Citing References" tab appears for each section of a statutory code. This list includes links to cases and secondary sources, such as *American Law Reports, Strong's North Carolina Index,* and law review articles that cite your section of the code. The History tab provides summaries of how the statute has changed over time and links to prior versions of the statute and legislative history documents when available. The "Context and Analysis" tab provides references to relevant statutes, regulations, and secondary sources selected by West editors.

KeyCite provides a different set of flags and symbols representing the editors' opinion of the validity of the statute. For a statute to merit a red flag, the statute may have been amended by a recent session law, superseded, or repealed. A court may have ruled that the statute is at least partly unconstitutional or unconstitutional as applied. More subtly, a court may recognize that a statute may have been repealed or held unconstitutional by implication. To merit a yellow flag, a statute may have been renumbered or moved within the code, or a court may have questioned the statute or decided that the statute is constitutionally limited in some aspect. Another possibility is that some proposed legislation or a recently enacted session law may affect the statute.

B. Using Shepard's on Lexis Advance to Update Statutes

Shepard's statute presentation is similar to that for cases. It defaults to the Citing Decisions tab, which has all of the filters discussed in Section II D of this chapter. The "Citing Law Reviews, Treatises, Annotated Statutes, Court Documents, Restatements, and other Secondary Sources" tab (usually displayed as "Citing Law Reviews, Treatises …") provides a list of all secondary source documents on Lexis Advance that cite your code section. The "Legislative History" tab currently lists the session laws that created or amended the code section.

Compared to its citation reports for cases, Shepard's does not provide as many symbols for statutes. Many of the editorial judgments concerning statutes are spelled out. Shepard's uses a red exclamation point for legislative or judicial changes affecting the statute. A yellow exclamation point suggests there may be pending legislation that would affect the statute.

C. Restricting Statutory Updates

When using either KeyCite or Shepard's, enter the narrowest section of the relevant code to retrieve the most focused citation information with the least amount of irrelevant information. Alternatively, to receive broader, more comprehensive results, it may be necessary to use a citation higher in the statutory hierarchy, for example a citation for the part or subchapter above the relevant section. The need to expand your results may initially be difficult to determine. It may be safer to retrieve a broader, more comprehensive citation report and then limit the results as necessary.

VII. Updating Other Legal Information

In addition to cases and statutes, other primary authority may also be updated using KeyCite and Shepard's. For example, the North Carolina Constitution, North Carolina rules of court, and North Carolina administrative rules may all be updated with citators. A number of secondary sources, such as law review articles, may also be updated with KeyCite and Shepard's.

Chapter 10

Researching North Carolina Court Rules and Rules of Ethics

In addition to the substantive law, many rules govern the practice of law. The supreme court or the legislature in each jurisdiction create or adopt the rules. These rules include procedural and appellate court rules, rules of evidence, and rules of professional conduct. The legal system and the practice of law would not be possible without these rules. Due to their importance, court rules and rules of ethics must be available to judges, lawyers, and other researchers.

A practicing attorney must often reconcile overlapping sets of rules about both procedure and ethics. She must ensure not only that her actions don't conflict with these rules, but also that she uses the rules in concert to her client's advantage. This reconciliation is accomplished by a conceptual understanding of the rules as well as ready access to the rules so that they may be researched when necessary.

This chapter will discuss researching rules relevant to the practice of law in North Carolina.

I. North Carolina Rules of Practice

A. Rules of Procedure

The North Carolina Constitution specifies that the North Carolina Supreme Court alone is responsible for drafting and adopting rules of procedure and practice for the appellate courts.[1] While the North Carolina General Assembly may make the rules of procedure and practice for the trial courts, the Assembly

---

1. N.C. Const. art. 4, § 13(2).

may also delegate this authority to the Supreme Court.[2] The General Assembly has delegated this authority, but also retained the constitutional right to alter, amend, or repeal any rule of procedure or practice adopted by the Supreme Court for the Superior or District Court Divisions.[3] In spite of that retained right, the creation and adoption of the rules of the practice of law in North Carolina is generally the purview of the Supreme Court.

The most commonly consulted rules are those that deal with the procedure in cases before North Carolina state courts (for example, the Rules of Civil Procedure) and the rules that govern what material and testimony can be introduced in courts, the Rules of Evidence. On occasion, an annotated copy of the rules may be more useful for researchers looking for explanatory drafting committee notes or summaries of cases interpreting each rule. Other occasions will require quick access to the actual text of the rules without the clutter of annotations. Some useful locations and research strategies for a selected group of court rules are described below.

1. North Carolina Rules of Civil Procedure

The source for North Carolina Rules of Civil Procedure with the best combination of stability, accessibility, and annotations is Chapter 1A of the North Carolina General Statutes, particularly one of the annotated versions, either General Statutes of North Carolina Annotated or West's North Carolina General Statutes Annotated. For research purposes, these versions are well annotated and indexed. The annotated codes may be accessed either in print or online at Lexis Advance or WestlawNext. Alternatively, the North Carolina General Statutes at the General Assembly website (www.ncleg.net) is conveniently and freely available but may not have been updated since the last legislative session and does not include helpful annotations.

In addition to these state-wide rules of civil procedure, which are applicable to every Superior and District Court in North Carolina, each court also may have its own local rules. Local rules may address such matters as arguing motions, conducting pre-trial or settlement conferences, local considerations involving discovery issues, or calendaring issues for hearings. The North Carolina Court System website has a page for local rules and forms where a researcher can select the local rules by county (www.nccourts.org/Courts/CRS/Policies/LocalRules/Default.asp).

---

2. *Id.*
3. *Id.*; N.C. Gen. Stat. § 7A-34.

2. North Carolina Rules of Appellate Procedure

An important source for the North Carolina Rules of Appellate Procedure is the "Annotated Rules of North Carolina" annual volume of LexisNexis's print version of the General Statutes of North Carolina Annotated. This annotated version of the rules is also available online at Lexis Advance in the North Carolina State and Federal Court Rules database, where it is searchable and browsable.

West's North Carolina General Statutes Annotated includes a useful, annotated set of the Rules of Appellate Procedure. WestlawNext provides the Rules in a searchable and browsable database called North Carolina Rules of Appellate Procedure. These rules are not annotated, but there is a list of all sources that cite the rule on the citing references tab. Although the Rules of Appellate Procedure on WestlawNext are not annotated, they are currently updated.

The most convenient access to the Rules of Appellate Procedure is through the North Carolina Administrative Office of Courts "Rules" website (www. aoc.state.nc.us/www/public/html/rules.htm). Although generally not as current as the rules updated on Lexis Advance or WestlawNext, and not annotated like the rules available from Lexis, you will find a free, relatively recent copy of the Rules of Appellate Procedure in PDF format, with any recent amendments separately posted.

B. Rules of Evidence

An excellent source for an authoritative, annotated version of the North Carolina Rules of Evidence is one of the annotated codes, LexisNexis's General Statutes of North Carolina Annotated or West's North Carolina General Statutes Annotated, available in print and online. The Rules of Evidence are incorporated into Chapter 8C of the code. The rules are annotated in the Lexis print and online versions, but not in the West print or online versions. For a free, unannotated version of the Rules of Evidence, use the General Assembly website (www.ncleg.net/gascripts/statutes/Statutes.asp).

C. Combined Sources of North Carolina Practice Rules

In addition to the specific locations for the selected rules above, several sources of North Carolina rules of practice combine many of the state's rules into one collection.

West publishes the North Carolina Rules of Court, State and Federal each year. This three-volume, softbound set is a convenient (although unannotated) edition of North Carolina rules. In addition to the rules mentioned above, this collection includes many more rules addressing legal procedures such as local court rules, guidelines for child support, rules for arbitration, and even rules for commissions such as the Dispute Resolution Commission or the North Carolina Industrial Commission.

The above-described, annual "Annotated Rules of North Carolina" volume of LexisNexis's General Statutes of North Carolina Annotated is another convenient gold mine of almost fifty sets of state and federal rules governing the practice of law in North Carolina. This set is also browsable on Lexis Advance.

WestlawNext includes a "North Carolina Rules" database with many of the same rules as described in the West pamphlet above. Generally, these rules are not annotated. See the database scope note for the necessary commands and abbreviations for all the rules in the database.

II. Federal Rules of Practice

The federal courts most relevant to North Carolina practice and research include the Western, Middle, and Eastern divisions of the United States District Court in North Carolina; the United States Court of Appeals for the Fourth Circuit; and the United States Supreme Court. Each of these courts has its own rules of procedure. At the trial level, district courts operate using rules such as the Federal Rules of Civil Procedure, the Federal Rules of Criminal Procedure, and the Federal Rules of Evidence. All of the Courts of Appeals operate with Federal Rules of Appellate Procedure. The Supreme Court follows its own Rules of the Supreme Court.

An excellent source for federal rules of practice, procedure and evidence is the United States Courts' "Rules" webpage (www.uscourts.gov/rules). The site also includes the latest information about pending rule changes and opportunities for comments on proposed rules.

The United States Code Service and United States Code Annotated are also good sources of federal rules. They are indexed and annotated, available in the print codes and also online at Lexis Advance and WestlawNext respectively. In the print version of the United States Code Service, an extensive collection of rules appears in volumes at the end of the series. In the United States Code Annotated, the Federal Rules of Civil Procedure, the Federal Rules of Evidence, the Federal Rules of Appellate Procedure, and the Rules of the Supreme Court of the United States are included along with others as an appendix to title 28. The Federal Rules of Criminal Procedure are part of an appendix to title 18.

The local court rules for each federal court are easily located at each court's website. For example, see the local rules for the United States District Court for the Western District of North Carolina at www.ncwd.uscourts.gov.

Finally, the three-volume West publication called North Carolina Rules of Court includes a federal rules volume with federal rules relevant to federal practice in North Carolina. These softbound books are issued each year.

III. North Carolina State Bar Rules, Rules of Ethics, and Ethics Opinions

The North Carolina Bar was established in 1933 with the goal of protecting the public and promoting the profession.[4] The state bar has a number of important, specific functions that control, monitor, and support the practice of law in North Carolina. Researching North Carolina State Bar and ethics information is critically important to law practice and will be discussed in the remainder of this chapter.[5]

A. Rules and Regulations for the North Carolina State Bar

The State Bar is responsible for examining applicants wishing to practice law in North Carolina through the development and use of the bar exam. After applicants pass the bar exam, the state bar requires licensed attorneys to attend classes each year and report their attendance to ensure continued learning about new legal developments.[6] The bar provides standards for specialization certification in several areas of law. In support of ethical behavior, the bar develops ethics rules, counsels lawyers individually as well as through the issuance of opinions, and provides attorney ethics training events. Any complaints of attorney misconduct are investigated and disciplinary actions, if appropriate, are determined by the bar. All of these activities, as well as the operation of the state bar organization, require rules for their fair and equitable administration.

---

4. 1933 N.C. Sess. Laws 313 (Chapter 210). The North Carolina Supreme Court approved the Certificate of Organization of the North Carolina State Bar in October 1933, 205 N.C. 853.
5. For a more detailed explanation of the State Bar, its services, and the location of older rules and decisions, see Chapter 10 of Scott Childs & Nick Sexton, *North Carolina Legal Research Guide* (2d ed. 2009).
6. Continuing legal education materials are covered in Chapter 3.

Although privately funded through dues, the state bar is an organ of the State of North Carolina. The rules governing the state bar, its organization, operation, and activities are the "Rules and Regulations for the North Carolina State Bar" and are codified in title 27, chapter 1 of the North Carolina Administrative Code. Because these rules are part of the Administrative Code, sources of the code and research strategies for its use from Chapter 8 will be relevant for researching state bar rules. The "Rules and Regulations for the North Carolina State Bar" are sometimes called the "Administrative Rules of the State Bar."

B. 2003 Revised Rules of Professional Conduct

Not to be confused with the Rules and Regulations for the North Carolina State Bar described above, the "Revised Rules of Professional Conduct" govern the ethical practice of law. A thorough understanding of the Revised Rules of Professional Conduct is mandatory for bar admission and a demonstration of that knowledge is required in a separate exam in addition to the bar examination of substantive law. These rules of professional ethics inform the daily practice of law. All lawyers need to research and consult the rules periodically to address issues as they arise. Table 10-1 loosely categorizes the rules by general topic.

Table 10-1. North Carolina Revised Rules of Professional Conduct

General Subject	Rule
Client-Lawyer Relationship	Rule 1.1–Rule 1.19
Lawyer as Counselor	Rule 2.1–Rule 2.4
Lawyer as Advocate	Rule 3.1–Rule 3.8
Transactions with Persons Other than Clients	Rule 4.1–Rule 4.4
Law Firms and Associates	Rule 5.1–Rule 5.7
Public Service	Rule 6.1–Rule 6.6
Information about Legal Services	Rule 7.1–Rule 7.5
Maintaining the Integrity of the Profession	Rule 8.1–Rule 8.5

Like the Rules and Regulations for the North Carolina State Bar, the Revised Rules of Professional Conduct are also in title 27 of the North Carolina Administrative Code. However, they are codified in chapter 2 of the title. Again, Chapter 8 of this book will be relevant for researching the rules of ethics, as they are part of the Administrative Code.

C. Finding the Rules

The state bar has an excellent website (www.ncbar.gov) providing free and convenient access to both the Rules and Regulations for the North Carolina State Bar as well as the Revised Rules of Professional Conduct. At this writing, the Rules link is available in the left hand column at the homepage.

Both the Rules and Regulations for the North Carolina State Bar as well as the Revised Rules of Professional Conduct are available from several other print sources. The annual "Annotated Rules of North Carolina" volume of LexisNexis's General Statutes of North Carolina Annotated includes both sets of rules. West also publishes North Carolina Rules of Court, State and Federal, the three-volume softbound set that contains the rules in a handy desktop version.

D. North Carolina Formal Ethics Opinions

Any member of the North Carolina State Bar may submit a question about legal ethics to the bar, by phone or in writing. The bar administrative staff might answer a phone question immediately. There are also three types of written responses to ethics questions submitted to the bar. Two types are less formal, Ethics Advisories and Ethics Decisions. The more important responses are called Formal Ethics Opinions. These opinions are initially considered and proposed by the Ethics Committee of the State Bar and become Formal Ethics Opinions when they are adopted by the State Bar Council.[7] They represent considered interpretation of the rules of ethics applied to a specific fact situation but thought to be widely applicable to the bar membership at large.

Formal Ethics Opinions are most easily found at the North Carolina State Bar website (www.ncbar.gov). The adopted Formal Ethics Opinions are found under the Ethics link on the left column at the homepage. The formal opinions are available back to 1997. They are browsable by citation or by title. The opinions are also keyword searchable. Proposed opinions are also posted at the website. Earlier selected opinions between 1997 and 1981 are also available at the site, although they are organized under a different scheme. WestlawNext and Lexis Advance include databases of North Carolina Formal Ethics Opinions with coverage back to 1986 and 1997, respectively. The coverage on Lexis Advance is part of the National Reporter on Legal Ethics & Professional Responsibility, which includes only selected opinions.

---

7. For more information about how the State Bar addresses ethics questions, see Childs & Sexton, *supra* note 5.

All of the opinions are republished each year in the annual State Bar Handbook. Another source for the opinions is the State Bar Journal, which publishes the full text of the proposed Formal Ethics Opinions and then prints a list of the opinions that are finally adopted.

E. North Carolina Bar Association

In addition to the State Bar, other organizations support the practice of law in North Carolina. The largest is the North Carolina Bar Association. Unlike the official North Carolina State Bar, the bar association is a voluntary organization and does not regulate the practice of law. One of the important benefits of bar association membership is free access to an online legal research service called Fastcase. Fastcase provides some access to primary law from North Carolina and a number of other states as well as some federal law. Currently, Fastcase is one of the few online sources for North Carolina Pattern Jury Instructions (the other is Casemaker).

IV. The American Bar Association and Legal Ethics

The American Bar Association is a voluntary organization and does not control the practice of law in any jurisdiction. The Association, however, has long been a supporter of attorney codes of ethics by developing, adopting, and promoting model codes. The current code is the ABA Model Rules of Professional Conduct. The Model Rules are available on Lexis Advance, WestlawNext, and Bloomberg Law in the Lawyers' Manual on Professional Conduct: Model Rules and Standards database. Only the WestlawNext version is annotated with cases from jurisdictions that have adopted the rules, but all of the versions include explanations of the rules and the reasoning behind their adoption. As North Carolina's ethic rules are based upon this version, the model rules are an important source of persuasive authority.

The ABA also issues Formal Ethics Opinions based upon the model rules. These opinions may be persuasive, particularly for those states such as North Carolina that have adopted rules similar to the ABA's Model Rules. Many of the opinions are available at the ABA's Center for Professional Responsibility website for a fee, where you may browse a subject index of the opinions. The opinions are also available in searchable databases on Lexis Advance and WestlawNext.

Epilogue

Revisiting the Research Process

I. Using a Research Process

A. The Basic Process of Legal Research

Chapter 2 described a basic legal research process as a linear task. The chapters of this book followed that process. This basic process is a safe, logical, and reasonable approach to legal research. It is highly recommended for new researchers as they learn about the law as well as the sources of information and how these sources are used together to find and understand the law. The basic process can also be useful for seasoned researchers when researching a new or complex area of law. See Table E-1 for a reminder of the basic legal research process.

Table E-1. Basic Legal Research Process

Step 1: Gather information and plan your research.

Step 2: Search secondary sources

Step 3: Search statutory law in annotated codes

Step 4: Search for case law, using specific case-finding tools

Step 5: Search administrative law

Step 6: Update primary authority with citators

There are many benefits derived from using the basic process. First and foremost, secondary sources highlighted in the process will almost always be a terrific starting point. Even 10 or 15 minutes invested in an appropriate secondary source can save you hours of weeding through irrelevant primary materials you would otherwise have retrieved due to your lack of effective search terms or general background understanding of the issue. Why painfully piece together your own basic understanding of the law when someone else has already done that job for you and recorded the results in a secondary source? One key to effective research using the basic process is to understand the strengths and weaknesses of the available secondary sources so that you can efficiently pick the most appropriate one to begin your research.

Another benefit from using the basic research process is the certainty that you have checked all the reasonable sources of law in a logical order without skipping anything. This checklist allows you to focus on analyzing the law rather than wondering whether there is a major gap in a haphazard research process.

B. An Advanced Process of Legal Research

While the basic process of legal research will almost always be a safe and effective approach, it might not always be the most efficient process for an experienced researcher. Each research project is unique, and you will start each project with varying amounts of information and understanding. You might have valid reasons for starting your process in a different place. For example, perhaps you already have a citation to a statute that you choose as your starting point. An annotated code might lead you to relevant cases or regulations. A

Figure E-1. Basic Legal Research Process

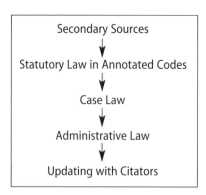

case citation to the "one good case" might lead you to the West Topic and Key Number System where you can find many related, relevant cases on your issue.

The diagram in Figure E-1 is a more accurate representation of a likely research process for a seasoned legal researcher. Notice that secondary sources are at the hub of the process connecting you to primary law. Secondary sources should still be your starting point unless you already have an excellent understanding of the area you are researching and significant citations to primary law. When starting with primary law, an annotated code would be a good choice because of its ability to connect to you to so much other information. Cases would generally be the next preferred primary law starting point. Administrative rules would be a last choice as a starting point unless you have a citation. If you do start with a citation to an administrative rule, because administrative rules are closely tied to their enabling act, it is often possible to locate the statutory authority cited at the end of a rule and work your way back to the annotated code.

Due to the interconnectedness of legal information, there are usually possibilities and options. The real question concerns efficiency. How can you get the information you need to zealously represent your client using the least amount of time and money? Develop a habit of working quickly, especially when selecting and using secondary sources. As valuable as they are, their value may be offset by the amount of time you spend with them.

II. Knowing When to Stop

One of the questions many new researchers have is knowing when to stop researching. The answer is that you know you have completed your research when you begin to see the same legal conclusion (perhaps found in a statute, a rule, or a group of cases) appearing in the different resources that you are using to research. But sometimes it is still difficult to stop researching and feel confident about your findings. This is particularly difficult if you feel that you did not find what you expected or perhaps did not find anything useful. By following the basic process outlined above and knowing that you exposed your search terms to all of the reasonable sources of law in a logical way, it is easier to have confidence that you found what there is to find.

Outside of the academic environment, there are additional considerations when deciding when to end your research. A lawyer's time is limited. There are also usually limits to the resources available for legal research as well as the amount of money that can be spent. Legal information is a commodity, and lawyers pay handsomely for it. These practical aspects of legal research must be balanced against the ethical and moral obligation to effectively research the law on behalf of your client. There can be no doubt that your duty to your client requires you to research efficiently but comprehensively.

III. Keeping Perspective

Life is complicated. Few things in life are simple, and situations are often not what they initially seem. Law school teaches students to keep an open mind, think critically, and examine things objectively. While legal issues are often complex, fortunately the process of legal research is not. Think about the kind of legal information that you will need to address your research topic. Do you expect the answer to be found in a statute, a case, or an administrative rule? Approach your research process with an understanding of the various sources of secondary and primary law and how those sources can interact and be used together.

Appendix A

North Carolina Routes of Appeal

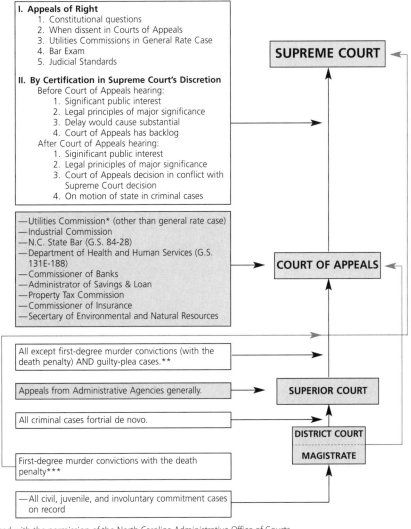

I. Appeals of Right
1. Constitutional questions
2. When dissent in Courts of Appeals
3. Utilities Commissions in General Rate Case
4. Bar Exam
5. Judicial Standards

II. By Certification in Supreme Court's Discretion
Before Court of Appeals hearing:
1. Significant public interest
2. Legal principles of major significance
3. Delay would cause substantial
4. Court of Appeals has backlog
After Court of Appeals hearing:
1. Siginificant public interest
2. Legal priniciples of major significance
3. Court of Appeals decision in conflict with Supreme Court decision
4. On motion of state in criminal cases

SUPREME COURT

— Utilities Commission* (other than general rate case)
— Industrial Commission
— N.C. State Bar (G.S. 84-28)
— Department of Health and Human Services (G.S. 131E-188)
— Commissioner of Banks
— Administrator of Savings & Loan
— Property Tax Commission
— Commissioner of Insurance
— Secretary of Environmental and Natural Resources

COURT OF APPEALS

All except first-degree murder convictions (with the death penalty) AND guilty-plea cases.**

Appeals from Administrative Agencies generally.

All criminal cases fortrial de novo.

First-degree murder convictions with the death penalty***

— All civil, juvenile, and involuntary commitment cases on record

SUPERIOR COURT

DISTRICT COURT

MAGISTRATE

Used with the permission of the North Carolina Administrative Office of Courts.

*   Appeals from agencies must be heard by Court of Appeals before Supreme Court.

**   Postconviction-hearing appeals and reviews of valuation of exempt property under G.S. Ch. 1C are final with Court of Appeals.

*** The only first-degree murder cases with direct appeal to the Supreme Court (tried after December 1, 1995) are those where defendant receives a sentence of death.

Appendix B

Geographic Boundaries of the United States Judicial System

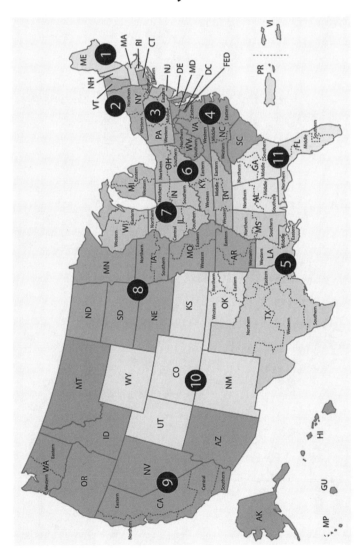

Map provided by the Administrative Office of the United States Courts at www.uscourts.gov/courtlinks. See that site for an interactive, color map that links to courts within each circuit.

Appendix C

Legal Citation[1]

A legal document must convince a lawyer or a judge reading it that its arguments were well researched and its analysis is well supported. One way legal writers do this is by providing references to the authorities used to develop that analysis and reach the conclusion. These references are called *legal citations*. They tell the reader where to find the authorities relied on and indicate the level of analytical support the authorities provide.[2] (See Table C-1.) In a legal document, every legal rule and every explanation of the law must be cited.

A legal researcher must be aware of and understand legal citation during the research process for two important reasons. First, citations convey critical information about the precedential value of an authority, making it easy for the researcher to know which cases to prioritize. For example, when working on a North Carolina law matter that is likely to end up in a North Carolina state court, a researcher should collect cases from North Carolina courts rather than federal or other states' courts. Conversely, when working on an issue governed by federal law, a researcher should gather federal cases and prefer cases from the federal jurisdiction where any litigation is likely to commence. In both examples, legal citations will tell the researcher the source of legal documents. Second, a researcher generally will create some sort of written document to summarize the research, which will include citations. To be efficient, the researcher should collect citation information in the research process. Otherwise, time will be wasted in the writing process retracing steps from the research process.

---

1. Portions of this appendix, especially Part III, are based on Suzanne E. Rowe, *Oregon Legal Research* (2d ed. 2007) and are used with the permission of the author.

2. ALWD & Darby Dickerson, *ALWD Citation Manual: A Professional System of Citation* 3 (4th ed. 2010).

Table C-1. Purposes of Legal Citation

- Show the reader where to find the cited material in the original case, statute, rule, article, or other authority.

- Indicate the weight and persuasiveness of each authority, for example, by specifying the court that decided the case, the author of a document, or the publication date of the authority.

- Convey the type and degree of support the authority offers, for example, by indicating whether the authority supports your point directly or only implicitly.

- Demonstrate that the analysis in your document is the result of careful research.

Source: *ALWD Citation Manual.*

Legal citations are included in the text of legal documents rather than being saved for a bibliography. While law students initially feel that these citations clutter documents, attorneys appreciate the valuable information that citations provide.

Of the many different citation systems that exist, this chapter addresses the most commonly used national citation manual, *The Bluebook: A Uniform System of Citation,*[3] as well as North Carolina citation rules. In law practice, you may encounter state statutes, court rules, and style manuals that dictate the form of citation used before the courts of different states. You may find that each firm or agency that you work for has its own preference for citation or makes minor variations to generally accepted format. Some law offices have their own style manuals, drawn from state rules and national manuals. Once you are aware of the basic function and format of citation, adapting to a slightly different set of rules is not difficult.

I. North Carolina Citation Rules

In North Carolina, the courts follow the *Bluebook*. The *Bluebook* requires that North Carolina Supreme Court and Court of Appeals decisions be cited

---

3. *The Bluebook: A Uniform System of Citation* (The Columbia Law Review Ass'n et al. eds., 19th ed. 2010) ("*Bluebook*").

to the regional reporter, *South Eastern Reporter, 2d*.[4] The *Bluebook* also acknowledges, however, that local rules may take precedence over *Bluebook* rules in documents submitted to North Carolina courts.[5] (Most states' courts have their own local rules of citation, and these rules differ somewhat from the rules of other states' courts and the rules in the *Bluebook*.) The few local citation rules for citing North Carolina judicial decisions to courts in North Carolina are contained in Appendix B of the *North Carolina Rules of Appellate Procedure*.

> Citations should be made according to the most recent edition of *A Uniform System of Citation [Bluebook]*. Citations to regional reporters shall include parallel citations to official state reporters.[6]

The result of these rules is that decisions from the North Carolina Supreme Court cited to courts in North Carolina must include citations to the official *North Carolina Reports* and the *South Eastern Reporter, 2d*. Decisions from the North Carolina Court of Appeals cited to courts in North Carolina must include citations to the official *North Carolina Court of Appeals Reports* and the *South Eastern Reporter, 2d*. Citation examples in *A Style Manual for the North Carolina Rules of Appellate Procedure* illustrate the Appendix B rules.[7] Examples of citations to judicial decisions are given in Table C-2.

Table C-2. Example Judicial Citations under North Carolina Rules

Supreme Court	*Rosi v. McCoy*, 319 N.C. 589, 356 S.E.2d 568 (1987).
Court of Appeals	*Mitchell v. Thornton*, 94 N.C. App. 313, 380 S.E.2d 146 (1989).
U.S. Supreme Court	*Brown v. Bd. of Educ.*, 349 U.S. 294 (1955).

---

4. *Bluebook* 258, Table T.1. Throughout this appendix, references will be provided to *Bluebook* pages and rule numbers in this fashion: *Bluebook* page number, Rule (or Table). Note that the rules are likely to remain the same in subsequent editions, though the page numbers will probably change.

5. *Bluebook* 30, Rule BT2.

6. *North Carolina Rules of Appellate Procedure*, Appendix B.

7. *A Style Manual for the North Carolina Rules of Appellate Procedure* (2012) is available at http://www.ncbar.org/media/28746809/appellatestylemanual_10152012.pdf. The most recent version of the style manual is always posted on the Office of the North Carolina Appellate Reporter's website at http://www.aoc.state.nc.us/www/public/html/ARResources.asp.

Lawyers practicing in North Carolina often follow the reporter parallel citation rules, even when they are not submitting documents to courts. If, however, the cases cited are not being submitted to court, and the writer chooses to cite only the *South Eastern Reporter, 2d*, then *Bluebook* Rule 10.4 requires the name of the court to be included in the citation so that the reader will know whether the case is from the supreme court or the court of appeals. The case citation examples from Table C-2 are presented in Table C-3 as required by Rule 10.4 when the official reporter is not cited.

Bluebook rules also establish citation standards for statutes and other rules in North Carolina as shown in Table C-4.

Table C-3. North Carolina Court Designations When Only Citing to Unofficial Reporters

Supreme Court	*Rosi v. McCoy*, 356 S.E.2d 568 (N.C. 1987).
Court of Appeals	*Mitchell v.Thornton*, 380 S.E.2d 146 (N.C. Ct. App. 1989).

Table C-4. Example North Carolina Statute and Rules Citations

Statute	N.C. Gen. Stat. § 20-16.3A (2013).
State Rules	8 N.C. Admin. Code 02 .0110 (2012) [North Carolina Administrative Rules]
	N.C. R. Civ. P. 12(b)(6). [North Carolina Rules of Civil Procedure]
Federal Rule	Fed. R. Evid. 802. [Federal Rules of Evidence]

II. Other States' Citation Rules

When working in another state, follow that state's local rules or use the format given in the *Bluebook* or another citation manual, depending on your supervisor's preferences. In the state of Washington, for example, the Office of Reporter of Decisions publishes a style sheet that determines citations to be used in documents submitted to Washington courts. The abbreviations required by that style sheet are familiar to lawyers practicing in Washington, but may be confusing to lawyers elsewhere.

III. The *Bluebook*

Student editors of four Ivy League law reviews have developed citation rules that are published as *The Bluebook: A Uniform System of Citation*, now in its 19th edition. As mentioned, the North Carolina Rules of Appellate Procedure (Appendix B) require use of the *Bluebook* for documents submitted to North Carolina courts with very few local rule adaptations. Additionally, an author submitting an article for publication in a law review that adheres to *Bluebook* rules, should follow *Bluebook* citation format.

For most of the last century, the *Bluebook* was the only national citation system that was widely recognized. Although law firms, agencies, and organizations consider *Bluebook* citations the norm, many practicing lawyers do not know its current rules; most assume that the *Bluebook* rules have not changed since they were in law school. Sections A and B below explain how to use the current *Bluebook* rules in writing memoranda and briefs. This section points out some areas of change from earlier editions of the *Bluebook*. Section C explains how to use the current *Bluebook* rules in writing articles for scholarly publication.

A. The *Bluebook*: Citations for Practice Documents

For practicing attorneys, the primary difficulty with the *Bluebook* is that it includes *two* citation systems: one for law review articles and another for legal memoranda and court documents. Most of the *Bluebook*'s over 500 pages are devoted to citations used for articles published in law journals. The rules most important to attorneys, those concerning legal memoranda and court documents, are given less attention in the *Bluebook* but are covered first below.

1. Reference Guide and Bluepages

Perhaps the most helpful information in the *Bluebook* is the reference guide on the inside back cover of the book, which gives examples of citations used in court documents and legal memoranda.[8] Another helpful portion of the

---

8. Examples of law review citations are found on the inside front cover of the *Bluebook*.

Bluebook appears on pages 3 through 51; these are the "Bluepages," which were introduced in the 18th edition. Previous editions contained a much shorter section called "Practitioner's Notes."

This section of Bluepages provides information for and additional examples of citations used in documents other than law review articles. The Bluepages list items that should be italicized or underlined in citations in legal memoranda and court documents. These include case names, titles of books and articles, and introductory signals. Items not included in the list should appear in regular type. Remember to follow the instructions in this list even when the *Bluebook* examples include large and small capital letters.

2. Index

The index at the back of the *Bluebook* is quite extensive, and in most instances it is more helpful than the table of contents. Most often, you should begin working with the *Bluebook* by referring to the index. Page numbers given in black type refer to citation instructions, while page numbers in blue refer to examples. Remember that the examples in the body of the *Bluebook* are in law review style. When writing a document other than a law review article, you will need to refer also to the practitioners' notes at the front of the book and the examples inside the back cover to see how you must modify the examples.

B. Incorporating Citations into a Document

A legal document must provide a citation for each idea that comes from a case, statute, article, or other source. Thus, paragraphs that state legal rules and explain the law should contain many citations. *Bluebook* 4-5, Rule B2.

A citation may offer support for an entire sentence or for an idea expressed in part of a sentence. If the citation supports the entire sentence, it is placed in a separate *citation sentence* that begins with a capital letter and ends with a period. *Bluebook* 4, Rule B2. If the citation supports only a portion of the sentence, it is included immediately after the relevant part of that sentence and set off from the sentence by commas in what is called a *citation clause*. *Bluebook* 4, Rule B2. Table C-5 provides examples of each.

Do not cite a client's facts or your conclusions about a case, statute, or other authority. The following sentence should not be cited: "Under the facts presented, our client's conduct would fall under first-degree burglary because a

---

Table C-5. Examples of Citation Sentences and Citation Clauses

---

Citation Sentences: First-degree trespass involves entering or remaining in a building of another without authorization. N.C. Gen. Stat. § 14-159.12 (2013). The term building is defined as "any structure or part of a structure, other than a conveyance, enclosed so as to permit reasonable entry through a door and roofed to protect it from the elements." N.C. Gen. Stat. § 14-159.11 (2013).

Citation Clauses: North Carolina statutes define both first-degree trespass, N.C. Gen. Stat. § 14-159.12 (2013), and second-degree trespass, N.C. Gen. Stat. § 14-159.13 (2013).

---

homeless family sometimes slept in the building he broke into." These facts and conclusions are unique to your situation and would not be found anywhere in the referenced source. (In a document to a court, however, you may need to cite to the record when citing these facts.)

C. Case Citations

A full citation to a case, whether you found it online or in print, includes (1) the name of the case, (2) the volume and reporter in which the case is published, (3) the first page of the case, (4) the exact page in the case that contains the idea you are citing (i.e., the *pinpoint* or *jump cite*), (5) the court that decided the case, and (6) the date the case was decided. *Bluebook* 7-15, Rule B4, and 87-99, Rule 10. The key points for citation to cases are given below, along with examples.

1. Essential Components of Case Citations

Include the name of just the first party on each side, even if several are listed in the case caption. If the party is an individual, include only the party's last name. If the party is a business or organization, shorten the party's name by using the abbreviations in Table 6. *Bluebook* 7, Rule B4.1.1. Recent editions of the *Bluebook* have changed the rule concerning the abbreviation of the first word of a party's name. Under earlier editions, the first word of a party's name could never be abbreviated, unless the name was a common abbreviation like NAACP, the National Association for the Advancement of Colored People. In the current edition, each word in a party's name that appears in Table T.6 is abbreviated in citations, even if it is the first word.

Between the parties' names, place a lower case "v" followed by a period. Do not use a capital "V" or the abbreviation "vs."

The parties' names may be italicized or underlined. Use the style preferred by your supervisor, and use that style consistently throughout each document. *Bluebook* 3, Introduction and Rule B1. Do not combine italics and underlining in one cite or within a single document.

Place a comma after the second party's name; do not italicize or underline this comma.

> EXAMPLE: *Harris v. Fla. Elections Comm'n*, 235 F.3d 578, 580 (11th Cir. 2000).

Next, give the volume and the reporter in which the case is found. Pay special attention to whether the reporter is in its first, second, or third series. Abbreviations for reporters are found in Table T.1 of the *Bluebook*. North Carolina reporters are included on page 258. In the example above, 235 is the volume number and F.3d is the reporter abbreviation for *Federal Reporter, Third Series.*

After the reporter name, include both the first page of the case and the pinpoint page containing the idea that you are referencing, separated by a comma and a space. *Bluebook* 9, Rule B4.1.2, and 67-69, Rule 3.2 The first page of the *Harris* case above is 578, and the page containing the specific idea being cited is 580. If the pinpoint page you are citing is also the first page of the case, then the same page number will appear twice even though this is repetitive.[9]

In a parenthetical following this information, indicate the court that decided the case, using abbreviations in Table T.1. *Bluebook* 10, Rule B4.1.3. In the above example, the Eleventh Circuit Court of Appeals, a federal court, decided the case.

If the reporter abbreviation clearly indicates which court decided a case, do not repeat this information in the parenthetical. To give two examples, only cases of the United States Supreme Court are reported in *United States Reports*,

---

9. When using an online version of a case, remember that a reference to a specific reporter page may change in the middle of a computer screen or a printed page. This means that the page number indicated at the top of the screen or printed page may not be the page where the relevant information is located. For example, if the notation *581 appeared in the text before the relevant information, the pinpoint cite would be to page 581, not page 580.

abbreviated U.S. Only cases decided by the North Carolina Court of Appeals are reported in *North Carolina Court of Appeals Reports,* which is abbreviated N.C. App. Repeating court abbreviations in citations to those reporters would be duplicative. By contrast, *South Eastern Reporter, 2d,* abbreviated S.E.2d, publishes decisions from different courts within several states, so the court that decided a particular case needs to be indicated parenthetically. Thus, in the last example below, "W. Va." indicates that the decision came from the West Virginia Supreme Court of Appeals rather than from another court whose decisions are also published in this reporter.

EXAMPLES: *Citizens United v. Fed. Election Comm'n,* 558 U.S. 310, 323 (2010).

     Mitchell v. Thornton, 94 N.C. App. 313, 316 (1989).

     Calacino v. McCutcheon, 356 S.E.2d 23, 25 (W. Va. 1987).

Note that these court abbreviations are not necessarily the same as postal codes. Abbreviating the West Virginia Supreme Court of Appeals as WV would be incorrect.

The final piece of required information in most cites is the date the case was decided. For cases published in reporters, give only the year of decision, not the month or date. Do not confuse the date of decision with the date on which the case was argued or submitted, the date on which a motion for rehearing was denied, or the publication date of the reporter. *Bluebook* 10, Rule B4.1.3, and 99, Rule 10.5. For cases that are unreported, give the month abbreviation, date, and year. *Bluebook* 11, Rule B4.1.4, and 99, Rule 10.5.

2. Full and Short Citations to Cases

The first time you mention a case by name, immediately give its full citation, including all of the information outlined above. Even though it is technically correct to include the full citation at the beginning of a sentence, a full citation takes up considerable space. By the time a reader gets through the citation and to your idea at the end of the sentence, the reader may have lost interest. The examples in Table C-6 demonstrate this problem.

After a full citation has been used once to introduce an authority, short citations are subsequently used to cite to this same authority. A short citation

Table C-6. Examples of Full Citations

Assume that this is the first time the case has been mentioned in this document.

CORRECT:	The law assumes that jurors in a trial will follow the judge's instructions and act in a rational fashion. *State v. Walker*, 356 S.E.2d 344, 346 (N.C. 1987).
CORRECT: (But should be avoided)	In *State v. Walker*, 356 S.E.2d 344, 346 (N.C. 1987), the court noted that the law assumes jurors in a trial will follow the judge's instructions and act in a rational fashion.

provides just enough information to allow the reader to locate the longer citation and find the pinpoint page. *Bluebook* 13-15, Rule B4.2, and 107-109, Rule 10.9.

When the immediately preceding citation is to the same source and the same page, use *id.* as the short cite. When the second cite is to a different page within the same source, follow the *id.* with "at" and the new pinpoint page number. Capitalize *id.* when it begins a citation sentence, just as the beginning of any sentence is capitalized. *Bluebook* 13, Rule B4.2, and 72-73, Rule 4.1. If the citation is from a source that is not the immediately preceding citation, give the name of one of the parties (generally the first party named in the full cite), the volume, the reporter, and the pinpoint page following "at." *Bluebook* 13, Rule B4.2, and 107-109, Rule 10.9. The North Carolina rules are demonstrated in the following example.

> EXAMPLE: A showing of adverse possession requires that a claimant be in actual and sole possession of the land with the intent to exclude others. *Mizzell v. Ewell*, 27 N.C. App. 507, 509, 219 S.E.2d 513, 515 (1975). The possession of the land must be demonstrated in the nature of an owner of the land and not just as an occasional trespasser. *Id.* at 510, 219 S.E.2d at 515. However, mere possession of the land does not establish ownership. *See id.* The possession must be hostile and without the permission of the previous owner. *State v. Brooks*, 275 N.C. 175, 180, 166 S.E.2d 70, 73 (1969). Additionally, the possession must be within the known and obvious boundaries of the property. *Mizzell*, 27 N.C. App. at 510, 219 S.E.2d at 515.

If you refer to the case by name in the sentence, your short citation does not need to repeat the case name, though lawyers often do. The last sentence of the example would also be correct as follows: "In *Mizzell,* possession within the known and obvious boundaries of the property was recognized as a basic requirement for the statutory meaning of possession. 27 N.C. App. at 510, 219 S.E.2d. at 515."

The format, *Mizzell* at 510, consisting of just a case name and page number, is incorrect. The volume and reporter abbreviation are also needed.

3. Prior and Subsequent History

Sometimes a citation needs to show what happened to a case at an earlier or later stage of litigation. The case you are citing may have reversed an earlier case, as in the example below. If you are citing a case for a court's analysis of one issue and a later court reversed only on the second issue, you need to alert your reader to that reversal. Or, if you decide for historical purposes to include in a document discussion of a case that was later overruled, your reader needs to know that as soon as you introduce the case. Prior and subsequent history can be appended to the full citations discussed above. *Bluebook* 12-13, Rule B4.1.6, and 101, Rule 10.7.

> EXAMPLE: The only time that the Supreme Court addressed the requirement of motive for an EMTALA claim, the court rejected that requirement. *Roberts v. Galen of Va.,* 525 U.S. 249, 253 (1999), *rev'g* 111 F.3d 405 (6th Cir. 1997).

D. Federal Statutes

The general rule for citing federal laws is to cite the *United States Code* (U.S.C.), which is the official code for federal statutes. In reality, that publication is published so slowly that the current language will most likely be found in a commercial code, either *United States Code Annotated* (published by West) or *United States Code Service* (published by LexisNexis). A cite to a federal statute includes the title, code name, section, publisher (except for U.S.C.), and date. The date given in statutory cites is the date of the print volume in which the statute is published, not the date the statute was enacted. If the language of a portion of the statute is reprinted in the pocket part, include the dates of both the bound volume and the pocket part. *Bluebook* 15-17, Rule B5, and 111-

125, Rule 12. If the language appears only in the pocket part, include only the date of the pocket part. *Bluebook* 115, Rule 12.3.2.

    EXAMPLE: (Statutory language appears in both the bound volume and the supplement):

                21 U.S.C.A. § 848 (West 1999 & Supp. 2013).

    EXAMPLE: (Statutory language appears in just the supplement):

                21 U.S.C.A. § 848(e)(2) (West Supp. 2013).

E. Signals

A citation must show the level of support each authority provides. You do this by deciding whether to use an introductory signal and, if so, which one. The more common signals are explained in Table C-7. Bluebook 54-59 R1.2.

Recent editions of the *Bluebook* have changed the rule on the use of the signal *see* back to the rule in force under the 15th and earlier editions. The current rule is that *see* is used only to show that the authority offers implicit support for an idea. Under the 16th edition, the signal *see* was used before virtually all citations. If you work for attorneys who attended law school while the 16th edition of the *Bluebook* was in use (1996–2000), they may not be familiar with the current rule.

Table C-7. Common Signals

No signal	• The source cited provides direct support for the idea in the sentence. • The cite identifies the source of a quotation.
See	• The source cited offers implicit support for the idea in the sentence. • The source cited offers support in dicta.
See also	• The source cited provides additional support for the idea in the sentence. • The support offered by *see also* is not as strong or direct as authorities preceded by no signal or by the signal see.
E.g.	• Many authorities state the idea in the sentence, and you are citing only one as an example; this signal allows you to cite just one source while letting the reader know that many other sources say the same thing.

F. Explanatory Parentheticals

At the end of a citation, you can append additional information about the authority in parentheses. Sometimes this parenthetical information conveys to the reader the weight of the authority. For example, a case may have been decided *en banc* or *per curiam*. Or the case may have been decided by a narrow split among the judges who heard the case. Parenthetical information also allows you to name the judges who joined in a dissenting, concurring, or plurality opinion. *Bluebook* 110, Rule 10.6.1. An explanatory parenthetical following a signal can convey helpful, additional information in a compressed space. *Bluebook* 59, Rule 1.5. When using this type of parenthetical, be sure that you do not inadvertently hide a critical part of the court's analysis at the end of a long citation, where a reader is likely to skip over it.

> EXAMPLE: Excluding relevant evidence during a sentencing hearing may deny the criminal defendant due process. *Green v. Georgia*, 442 U.S. 95, 97 (1979) (per curiam) (regarding testimony of co-defendant's confession in rape and murder case).

G. Quotations

Quotations should be used only when the reader needs to see the text exactly as it appears in the original authority. Of all legal audiences, trial courts are probably most receptive to longer quotations. For example, quoting the controlling statutory language can be extremely helpful. As another example, if a well known case explains an analytical point in a particularly insightful way, a quotation may be warranted.

Excessive quotation has two drawbacks. First, quotations interrupt the flow of your writing when the style of the quoted language differs from your own. Second, excessive use of quotations may suggest to the reader that you do not fully comprehend the material; it is much easier to cut and paste together a document from pieces of various cases than to synthesize and explain a rule of law. Quotations should not be used simply because you cannot think of another way to express an idea.

When a quotation is needed, the words, punctuation, and capitalization within the quotation marks must appear *exactly* as they are in the original. Treat a quotation as a photocopy of the original text. Any alterations or omissions must be indicated. Include commas and periods inside quotation marks; place other punctuation outside the quotation marks unless it is included in the original text. *Bluebook* 76-79, Rule 5. Also, try to provide smooth transitions between your text and the quoted text. If a quotation is more than 50 words, it must appear in a block quote (indenting the text on both the right and left sides). *Bluebook* 76, Rule 5.1.

H. Citation Details

The following citation details deserve special note because they frequently trip up novices.

- Use proper ordinal abbreviations. The most confusing are 2d for "Second" and 3d for "Third" because they differ from the standard format. *E.g.*, *Bluebook* 97, Rule 10.4(a).

- Do not insert a space between abbreviations of single capital letters. For example, there is no space in U.S. Ordinal numbers like 1st, 2d, and 3d are considered single capital letters for purposes of this rule. Thus, there is no space in S.E.2d or F.3d because 2d and 3d are considered single capital letters. Leave one space between elements of an abbreviation that are not single capital letters. For example, F. Supp. 2d has a space on each side of "Supp." It would be incorrect to write F.Supp.2d. *E.g.*, *Bluebook* 10, Rule B4.1.3

- In citation sentences, abbreviate case names, court names, months, and reporter names. Do not abbreviate these words when they are part of textual sentences unless the abbreviations are "widely known"; instead, spell them out as in the example below. *Bluebook* 91, Rule 10.2.1(c), and 94, Rule 10.2.2.

EXAMPLE: The Ninth Circuit held that Oregon's Measure 11 did not violate constitutional rights provided under the Eighth and Fourteenth Amendments. *Alvarado v. Hill*, 252 F.3d 1066, 1069-70 (9th Cir. 2001).

- When *id.* is used to show support for just part of a sentence, this short cite is set off from the sentence by commas and is not capitalized. *See Bluebook* 72-73, Rule 4.1.

- It is most common in legal documents to spell out numbers zero through ninety-nine and to use numerals for larger numbers. However, always spell out a number that is the first word of a sentence. *Bluebook* 81, Rule 4.1.

I. The *Bluebook*: Citations for Law Review Articles

Using the *Bluebook* to write citations for law review articles is considerably easier than using it for practice documents. As noted above, almost all of the examples given in the *Bluebook* are in law review format. Table C-8 of this chapter summarizes the typeface used for several common sources and gives examples.

Table C-8. *Bluebook* Typeface for Law Review Footnotes

Item	Type Used	Example
Cases	Use ordinary type for case names in full citations. (See text for further explanation.)	Legal Servs. Corp. v. Velazquez, 531 U.S. 533 (2001).
Books	Use large and small capital letters for the author and the title.	DAVID S. ROMANTZ & KATHLEEN ELLIOTT VINSON, LEGAL ANALYSIS: THE FUNDAMENTAL SKILL (2d ed. 2009).
Periodical articles	Use ordinary type for the author's name, italics for the title, and large and small capitals for the periodical.	Adell Louise Amos, *The Use of State Instream Flow Laws for Federal Land: Respecting State Control While Meeting Federal Purposes*, 36 ENVIR. LAW 1237 (2006).
Explanatory phrases	Use italics for all explanatory phrases, such as *aff'g, cert. denied, rev'd,* and *overruled by.*	Legal Servs. Corp. v. Velazquez, 531 U.S. 533 (2001), *aff'g* 164 F.3d 757 (2d Cir. 1999).
Introductory signals	Use italics for all introductory signals, such as *see* and e.g. when they appear in citations, as opposed to text.	*See id.*

Law review articles place citations in footnotes or endnotes, instead of placing citations in the main text of the document. *Bluebook* 53, Rule 1.1(a). Most law review footnotes include text in ordinary type, in italics, and in large and small capital letters. *Bluebook* 56, Rule 2.2(a). This convention is not universal, and each law review selects the typefaces it will use. Some law reviews may use only ordinary type and italics. Others may use just ordinary type. *Bluebook* 62-64, Rule 2.1.

The typeface used for a case name depends on (1) whether the case appears in the main text of the article or in a footnote and (2) how the case is used. When a case name appears in the main text of the article or in a textual sentence of a footnote, it is italicized. By contrast, if a footnote contains an embedded citation, the case name is written in ordinary text. Similarly, when a full cite is given in a footnote, the case name is written in ordinary type. But when a short cite is used in footnotes, the case name is italicized. Assuming you are submitting an article to a law review that uses all three typefaces, *Bluebook* Rule 2 dictates which typeface to use for each type of authority.

Law review footnotes use short cites generally the same as in other documents. The short cite *id.* can be used only if the preceding footnote contains only one authority. *Bluebook* 72-73, Rule 4.1. One unique *Bluebook* requirement is the "rule of five." This rule states that a short cite *id.* can be used if the source is "*readily found in one of the preceding five footnotes.*" *Bluebook* 107, Rule 10.9 (cases) (emphasis in original); *Bluebook* 113, Rule 12.9 (statutes).

IV. *ALWD Citation Manual*

Another national citation manual, the *ALWD Citation Manual*, was initially published in 2000 by a professional organization of legal writing professors. The fifth edition is scheduled for publication in 2014 under a modified title, *ALWD Guide to Legal Citation*.[10] It is not covered here because the newest edition makes significant changes the structure of the guide and the resulting citations but was not available as this book went to print.

Although North Carolina courts generally follow the *Bluebook* and a few local rules, the *ALWD Guide* is the best citation manual for novices to begin understanding legal citation. The guide uses just one set of rules (not different rules for practice documents than for law review articles), explanations are

---

10. Coleen Barger & ALWD, *ALWD Guide to Legal Citation* (5th ed. 2014).

clear, and the examples are useful to both law students and practicing attorneys. The citations that are created are similar to those created by the *Bluebook* for practice documents.

V. Editing Citations

To be sure that the citations in a document correctly reflect your research and support your analysis, include enough time in the writing and editing process to check citation accuracy. While writing the document, refer frequently to the local rules or to the citation guide required by your supervisor. After you have completely finished writing the text of the document, check the citations carefully again. Be sure that each citation is still accurate after all the writing revisions you have made. For example, moving a sentence might require you to change an *id.* to another form of short cite, or vice versa. In fact, some careful writers do not insert *id.* citations until they are completely finished writing and revising.

Sometimes editing for citations can take as long as editing for writing mechanics. The time invested in citations is well spent if it enables the person reading your document to quickly find the authorities you cite and to understand your analysis.

About the Authors

Scott Childs is a graduate of the University of Alabama School of Law and the Florida State University School of Library and Information Studies. He practiced law with the Legal Services Corporation of Alabama before joining the staff and teaching legal research as a librarian at Cornell Law School, Louisiana State University Law Center, and the University of North Carolina School of Law, where he was the Deputy Director of the Law Library and Clinical Professor of Law. He currently serves as Associate Professor and Associate Dean for Library and Technology Services at the University of Tennessee College of Law.

Sara Sampson earned her J.D. from The Ohio State University College of Law and her M.L.I.S from Kent State University. She is currently the Deputy Director of the Law Library and Clinical Assistant Professor of Law at the University of North Carolina at Chapel Hill. Before arriving at UNC, Sampson worked at Georgetown University as the Head of Reference and an adjunct professor teaching Legal Research Skills for Practice, Advanced Legal Research, and Introduction to Scholarly Note Writing. Sampson was also a reference librarian and adjunct legal writing professor at Ohio State. Additionally, she spent five years as a judicial law clerk to two judges on the Ohio Fourth District Court of Appeals.

Index

A Style Manual for the North Carolina Rules of Appellate Procedure, 177

Accuracy of information in formats, 17

Administrative agencies, 127–131, 135, 140, 171

Administrative law, 23, 64, 127–129, 131–133, 135, 137, 140, 169, 170
  Administrative law judges, 131
  Code of Federal Regulations (CFR), 136–138
  Federal administrative decisions, 127, 135, 136, 140
  Federal administrative regulations, 127, 132, 135–138
  Federal, generally, 55, 95, 136
  Federal Register, 135–140
  North Carolina, generally, 83, 85, 90, 98, 160, 162, 190
  North Carolina Administrative Code, 64, 129–136, 164, 178
  North Carolina administrative decisions, 64, 98, 127, 129–131, 134, 135, 140
  North Carolina administrative rules, 127–135, 137, 161, 164, 178
  North Carolina Register, 128–130, 133, 134, 137

Advance sheets, 102, 112

Age of information in formats, 17

ALWD Citation Guide, 9, 23, 190

American Bar Association, 166

American Bar Association Formal Ethics Opinions, 166

American Bar Association Model Rules of Professional Conduct, 166

American Constitutional Law, 85

American Jurisprudence (Am Jur), 36, 38, 52

American Jurisprudence Legal Forms, 52

American Law Institute, 48, 50

American Law Reports, 29, 34, 46, 62, 63, 113

American Law Reports, Federal, 46, 63

Atlantic Reporter, 109, 115

Attorney general opinions, 63, 134–135, 141
  North Carolina, 63, 134–135
  United States, 141

Availability of information formats, 15–16

BCite, 154, 155

Bill tracking, 78–85, 90–93
  Federal, 90–93
  North Carolina, 141

Bills, federal, 90–93

Bills, North Carolina, 61–62, 78–85
  Chronology, 83, 84, 86–88
  Enrolled, 91
  Floor debate, 88, 91
  Generally, 61–62, 78–85
  Ratified, 61–62, 81, 83

Versions, 81–83
Black's Law Dictionary, 98
Blogs, 34, 54
Bloomberg Law, 23, 26, 57, 65, 67, 68, 70, 71, 73–75, 84, 93, 103, 105, 120, 125, 126, 129–131, 133, 134, 137, 138, 140, 141, 154, 166
Bluebook, A Uniform System of Citation, 9, 23, 67, 109, 140, 175–190
Boolean searching, 25–26, 29, 97

California Reporter, 109
Case notes, 64, 69
Casemaker, 15, 53, 166
Chaptered bills, 81, 83
Citations to cases, 183–187
Citator, *See* BCite, KeyCite, Shepard's, Updating
Code of Federal Regulations (*CFR*), 136–138
Committee minutes, 79, 80, 86–88, 96
Compiled legislative history, 94, 95
Confidentiality of information formats, 18
Congressional Record, 91, 92, 95, 96
Congress.gov, 92–95
Constitutional interpretation, 59–60
Context of information within formats, 17–18
Continuing legal education (CLE), 34, 50–51, 163
Corpus Juris Secundum (*CJS*), 39
Cost of information formats, 16–17
Current Law Index, 43

Daily Bulletin, 84, 85
Dealmaker, 52
Descriptive-Word Index, 36, 117
Digests, 12, 18–19, 24, 29–31, 72, 102, 107, 114–125
Atlantic Digest, 115

Descriptive-Word Index, 36, 117
Headnotes, 97, 101, 102, 104, 107, 112, 114, 115, 117–121, 124, 125, 149
North Carolina Digest, 114–116, 119
North Western Digest, 115
Online, 120–122, 123
Pacific Digest, 115
South Eastern Digest, 115
Table of cases, 36, 119
Topics and Key Numbers, 114–115, 117, 119–121
Words and Phrases, 120
Disposition, 59, 72, 102, 107, 113, 150
Docket number, 106
Douglas' Forms, 51, 52

e-CFR, 136–137, 138
Efficiencies among information formats, 18
Enabling statute, 127, 132, 169
Encyclopedias, 6, 11, 18, 34, 35, 36–39, 46, 59, 62, 72, 113, 117
Enrolled bills, 81, 91
Ethics opinions, 163, 165, 166
American Bar Association Formal Ethics Opinions, 166
North Carolina Formal Ethics Opinions, 165, 166

Fastcase, 15, 23, 53, 103, 104, 110, 120, 166
Federal administrative law, *See* Administrative law
Federal Appendix, 110–112
Federal Cases, 110, 111
Federal Digital System (FDsys), 59, 71, 72, 90, 96, 136, 137, 138, 139
Federal judicial system, geographic boundaries, (Appendix B), 173

Federal Register, 135–140
Federal Reporter, 110–112, 182
Federal Rules Decisions, 110, 111
Federal Rules of Appellate Procedure, 111–113, 162
Federal Rules of Civil Procedure, 111, 162
Federal Rules of Evidence, 111, 162, 178
Federal Rules of Practice, 162–163, 178
Federal Supplement, 110, 111, 188
Field searching, 28, 120, 133
FindLaw Legal News, 45
Forms, 34, 51–52, 160

General Assembly, 19, 61–65, 79, 84, 86–89, 128, 129, 134, 159, 160
General Statutes of North Carolina, 6, 19, 24, 25, 28, 36, 57, 59, 62–65, 67, 84, 86, 96, 132, 160–162, 165
General Statutes of North Carolina Advance Annotation Service (AAS), 63
General Statutes of North Carolina Advance Legislative Service (ALS), 63
Generating research terms (*see also* Journalistic and TARPP), 11, 13–14, 31, 33
Google Scholar, 45
Government Printing Office (GPO), 71, 90, 96, 136, 137, 138
Gubernatorial statements, 89, 90

Headnotes, 31, 97, 101, 102, 104, 107, 112, 114, 121, 124, 125, 145, 149, 153, 157
HeinOnline, 44, 46, 62, 94, 137
Hornbooks, 40
House calendar, North Carolina, 79

House Journal, North Carolina, 80, 86, 87–88, 90, 96
House of Representatives, North Carolina, 78
House of Representatives, United States, 90, 91
"How Our Laws Are Made," 90
Index to Legal Periodicals and Books (ILP), 43

Journalistic method of developing search terms, 66
Jurisdiction, 7, 9, 13, 98–100
Jury instructions, 34, 52–53, 166

KeyCite, 12, 140, 144, 145, 150–154, 157, 158
Keyword searching, 21–22, 25–29, 67, 75, 115, 120, 122, 132, 137, 138, 148, 153

Legal analysis, 1, 3–4, 20, 34, 42, 175, 176
Legal periodicals, 41–46
Legal Resources Index (LRI), 43
LegalTrac, 43
Legislative process, 78–84, 90
  Federal, 90
  North Carolina, 78–84
Legislative Services Commission, 79
Legislative Week in Review, 84
Lexis, 21–38, 41, 44, 46, 51, 52, 63, 69, 71, 83, 84, 103, 105, 107, 110, 123–125, 147, 152, 161
Lexis Advance, 24, 26, 27, 57, 63, 64, 67, 68, 83, 90, 93, 94, 120, 123–125, 129, 130, 133, 134, 137, 138, 140, 145, 158, 160, 161, 166
List of Sections Affected, 138, 139
Loislaw, 15, 23, 103, 104, 110, 120

Mandatory authority, 4–6, 11, 33, 108, 156
Mecklenburg Declaration of Independence, 56
Mecklenburg Resolves, 55, 56

National Conference of Commissioners on Uniform State Laws, 53
National Law Journal, 45
Natural language searching, 25, 29, 38, 133
New York Law Journal, 45
New York Supplement, 109
North Carolina Administrative Code, 64, 129–136, 164, 178
North Carolina Administrative Office of Courts, 8, 52, 104, 171
North Carolina Attorney General Opinions, 63, 134–135
North Carolina Bar, 45, 51, 163–164
North Carolina Bar Association, 15, 23, 53, 104, 166
North Carolina Bar Journal, 45
North Carolina Cases, 102
North Carolina Constitution, 5, 6, 23, 36, 55–59, 99, 159
North Carolina Court of Appeals, 8, 19, 97–101, 108
North Carolina Court of Appeals Reports, 101, 144, 177, 185
North Carolina Digest, 114–116, 119, 120
North Carolina District Court, 7, 98–100, 110, 160
North Carolina Formal Ethics Opinions, 165–166
North Carolina Lawyers Weekly, 45
North Carolina Legislative Service, 63, 64

North Carolina Office of Administrative Hearings, 129, 130, 131, 133
North Carolina Pattern Jury Instructions, 53, 166
North Carolina Register, 128–130, 133, 134, 137
North Carolina Reports, 101, 106, 119, 144, 157, 177, 183
North Carolina Routes of Appeal, (Appendix A), 171
North Carolina Rules of Appellate Procedure, 108, 159, 161, 177, 179
North Carolina Rules of Civil Procedure, 160, 178
North Carolina Rules of Court, State and Federal, 161, 165
North Carolina Rules of Evidence, 159, 161, 178
North Carolina Session Laws, 62, 64, 71, 86, 87, 96
North Carolina Superior Court, 7, 8, 53, 98, 131, 160
North Carolina Supreme Court, 6, 97–99, 101, 104–106, 115, 159, 160, 163, 176–178
North Eastern Reporter, 109
North Western Reporter, 109, 115
Notes of Decisions, 64, 69
Nutshells, 39, 40

Opinion, 6–7, 19, 31, 45, 57, 97–126, 131, 134–135, 141, 146, 156, 165–166, 189

PACER, 113
Pacific Reporter, 109, 115
Parallel citations, 106, 177, 178
Periodicals, *See* Legal periodicals
Persuasive authority, 5, 6, 108, 166

Pocket parts, 20–21, 37, 38, 39, 47, 50, 64, 73, 117–118, 139, 143, 185–186

Popular name, 20, 64–67, 73, 74, 91, 95

Practice materials, 50–53

Practising Law Institute, 51

Primary authority, 4–6, 127

Private laws, 71

ProQuest, 95

Public laws, 71, 74, 91, 94, 95

Ratification, 55, 58, 61, 62, 81, 83

Ratified bills, 81–83

Reading clerk, 79

Regional reporters, 101, 109, 115, 177

Restatements, 35, 48–50, 147, 158

Revised Rules of Professional Conduct, 164, 165

Rules and Regulations for the North Carolina State Bar, 163–165

Rules of North Carolina, 63, 161–162, 165

Secondary authority, 5, 6

Secondary source characteristics, 35

Secondary sources, Traditional, 36–50

Segment searching, 28, 120, 133

Senate, 78, 91
   North Carolina, 78
   United States, 91

Senate calendar, North Carolina, 79

Senate Journal, North Carolina, 80, 86, 87–88, 90, 96

Session laws, 61–65, 67, 71, 81, 86, 87, 91, 93, 95, 96

Shepard's North Carolina Citations, 144

Shepard's South Eastern Reporter Citations, 144

Signals, 180, 186, 189

Small Claims Court, 98

South Eastern Digest, 102, 107, 115

South Eastern Reporter, 101, 102, 105–107, 118, 144, 177, 178, 183, 188

South Western Reporter, 109

Southern Reporter, 109

Stare decisis, 98, 100

Statutes at Large, 71, 72, 91, 95, 96

Statutory interpretation, 70, 85

Strong's North Carolina Index, 36, 38, 64, 157

Study reports, 79, 86, 88–89, 96

Subsequent history, 146, 155, 185

Symbols used by citators
   BCite, 154, 155
   Generally, 145
   KeyCite, 150–154
   Shepard's, 144–148

Synopsis, 97, 104, 107

TARPP method of developing search terms, 66

Terms and connectors searching, 25–29, 67, 97, 123

THOMAS, 92

Topic searching, 119, 120–125

Topics and Key Numbers, 114–115, 117, 119–121

Treatises, 6, 11, 19, 24, 35, 39–41, 52, 59, 132, 147, 158

Uniform Laws Annotated (ULA), 54

United States Attorney General Opinions, 141

United States Code, 58, 59, 71–75, 91, 94–96, 136–138, 162, 185

United States Code Annotated, 58, 59, 72–74, 94, 96, 137, 162, 185

United States Code Service, 58, 59, 72–74, 96, 136–138, 162, 185

United States Constitution, 55, 58, 59

United States Courts of Appeals, 8–9, 99–100, 110, 162

United States District Courts, 8, 99, 100, 110, 112, 162

United States Reports, 110–112, 182

United States Supreme Court, 9, 100, 110–113, 162, 179, 182

United States Supreme Court Reports, Lawyers' Edition, 110, 112

Unpublished opinions, 108, 111, 113

Updating, 35, 73, 133, 138–140, 143, 145, 148, 150, 154, 157, 158
Administrative law, 133, 138–140
Generally, 143–158, 168
Statutes, 73, 157–158

VersusLaw, 23, 103, 104, 110, 112, 120

Veto, 81, 90, 91

West Legal Forms, 52

West's North Carolina General Statutes Annotated, 21, 57, 59, 63, 64, 67, 86, 96, 132, 165

West's Supreme Court Reporter, 112

Westlaw, 18, 21–23, 24, 38, 39, 41, 43, 44, 46, 51, 52, 54, 62, 64, 65, 71, 103, 107, 110, 114, 121, 144

WestlawNext, 24, 26–28, 30, 57, 64, 67–69, 71, 74, 75, 83, 87, 90, 93, 94, 105, 106, 120–122, 124, 129–131, 133, 134, 137, 138, 140, 150, 151, 154, 160–162, 165, 166

Wikipedia, 17

Words and phrases, 37, 120